# Talkin Classroo

## Shaping Children's Learning Through Oral Language Instruction

Patricia G. Smith

Royal Melbourne Institute of Technology, Bundoora, Victoria, Australia

*Editor*

INTERNATIONAL
**Reading
Association**

800 Barksdale Road, PO Box 8139
Newark, Delaware 19714-8139, USA
www.reading.org

The International Reading Association attempts, through its publications, to provide a forum for a wide spectrum of opinions on reading. This policy permits divergent viewpoints without implying the endorsement of the Association.

**Director of Publications**  Joan M. Irwin
**Editorial Director, Books and Special Projects**  Matthew W. Baker
**Special Projects Editor**  Tori Mello Bachman
**Permissions Editor**  Janet S. Parrack
**Associate Editor**  Jeanine K. McGann
**Production Editor**  Shannon Benner
**Editorial Assistant**  Pamela McComas
**Publications Coordinator**  Beth Doughty
**Production Department Manager**  Iona Sauscermen
**Art Director**  Boni Nash
**Supervisor, Electronic Publishing**  Anette Schütz-Ruff
**Electronic Publishing Specialist**  Cheryl J. Strum
**Electronic Publishing Assistant**  John W. Cain

**Project Editor**  Jeanine K. McGann

**Cover Art**  Kathleen King

**Library of Congress Cataloging–in–Publication Data**
Talking classrooms : shaping children's learning through oral language instruction / Patricia G. Smith, editor.
     p.    cm.
Includes bibliographical references and index.
    ISBN 0-87207-278-9
    1. Language arts (Elementary).   2. Oral communication.   3. Communication in education   I. Smith, Patricia G.
LB1576 .T2293    2000
372.62'2–dc21                                                                    00-011376

Margaret Forster
Senior Research Fellow
Australian Council for Educational Research
Camberwell, Victoria, Australia

Jennifer Funke
Classroom Teacher/Researcher
Independent Consultant
Tempe, Arizona, USA

Dale Gordon
Consultant to Schools, Lecturer, Writer
Gisborne, Victoria, Australia

Patrick Griffin
Chair (Educational Assessment); Director, Assessment Research Centre; and
Head, Department of Learning and Educational Development
Faculty of Education
The University of Melbourne
Melbourne, Victoria, Australia

Susan Hill
Associate Professor, Early Childhood Education
University of South Australia
Underdale, South Australia, Australia

George Hunt
Lecturer in Language in Education, School of Education
University of Reading
Reading, United Kingdom

Gloria Latham
Lecturer in Literacy and Drama
RMIT University
Bundoora, Victoria, Australia

Stacy King Medd
ESL Instructor, K–6, Horace Mann Elementary School
Iowa City Community Schools
Iowa City, Iowa, USA

Bridie Raban
Mooroolbeek Foundation Chair of Early Childhood Education
The University of Melbourne
Melbourne, Victoria, Australia

Brian J. Richards
Professor of Education
University of Reading
Reading, United Kingdom

Patricia G. Smith
Senior Lecturer; Faculty of Education, Language, and Community Services
Royal Melbourne Institute of Technology
Bundoora, Victoria, Australia

Frank Serafini
Doctoral Candidate
Arizona State University
Scottsdale, Arizona, USA

Rebecca Willey
Primary Classroom Teacher
Glendale, Arizona, USA

Kathryn F. Whitmore
Associate Professor
The University of Iowa
Iowa City, Iowa, USA

Talking classrooms have not always been the norm. One's success as a teacher was once measured by the quietness of one's students. The teacher's voice was the predominant sound as she or he asked questions and gave monologues. Students were relegated to the role of passive consumers of knowledge rather than active learners (Barnes, 1976; Mehan, 1979). Now, our classrooms are full of the sounds of students talking. We consciously promote active learning through talk. The questions to be asked now center around the broad themes of how and why talk in classrooms has changed, what models of classroom talk should look like, and the most effective methods of assessing talk that is volatile, dynamic, and interactive without destroying that which is being assessed. The following chapters are structured to develop these broad themes, following a progression in emphasis from the philosophical and theoretical background in the first chapters through the methods and models of talk in classrooms in subsequent chapters, and finishing with discussions of assessment in the final chapters.

The question of why talk in classrooms has changed is addressed through a review of language and thought using a broad philosophical perspective in Chapters One through Three. Particular attention is paid to the work of Vygotsky (1962, 1978) and Bakhtin (1981) in Chapters One and Two. Vygotsky wrote that language is the crucial link between the social and psychological planes of human functioning. Language is the tool of the mind used by individuals to transform the external world and construct their own internal mental processes by collaborating with others in meaningful social activities. The learner uses private self-directed speech to guide his or her speaking.

For Bakhtin, language is never a monologue; it is a dialogue. We meet the world through signs called words and because these signs are always someone else's as well as our own, we meet the world through dialogue. This cothinking is the foundation of our consciousness. Our students must discover that as Bakhtin (1981) believes,

> The word in language is half someone else's. It becomes "one's own" only when the speaker populates it with his own intention, his own accent, when he appropriates the word, adapting it to his own semantic and expressive intention. (pp. 293–294)

Many of the authors in this volume describe classrooms where learners use language for a variety of purposes—they speculate, predict, listen, organize, critique, persuade, report, and evaluate. This gives a practical focus to the ideas of Vygotsky, Bakhtin, and other language theorists, starting from the premise that language is a sign system that allows us to structure, regulate, and give meaning to our world. Barnes, Britton, and Torbe (1986) argue that classrooms must become places where students are given time to hypothesize and shape their understandings through talk. They found that the learner's talk is marked by frequent hesitations, rephrasings, false starts, and changes in direction. Chapters Four, Six, and Seven contain extensive examples of students using this kind of "exploratory talk."

We are reminded that we should not forget that imaginative language, the affective and aesthetic dimension, is at the heart of learning. Building conversations in the classroom is a means toward furthering young children's critical thinking and building a thoughtful community of learners. Chapter Five provides a multitude of practical suggestions for teachers who want to keep their students' curiosity alive, while Chapter Eight shows the opportunities that can be lost when adults unwittingly extinguish children's creative fire.

Oral language assessment is particularly considered in the final two chapters, although it is an integral part of the discussion in previous chapters as well. An exploratory use of the American literacy profiles on a small, localized scale in Chapter Nine provides a contrast to the large, Australian national survey project used for assessment in Chapter Ten. Both assessment chapters share a focus on capturing for assessment purposes the volatile nature of talk, and on interpreting that talk as holistically as possible. Above all, assessment practices must not harm, but rather must encourage the individual's confidence in his or her worth to society.

Edited collections are often criticized because there is dissonance. However, this collection has deliberately chosen to be multivoiced. The authors present a variety of vignettes, practical suggestions, empirical reports, and research results that show how authentic language and thought processes can be applied through talk in classrooms. Each chapter reinforces the holistic view of language processes and creates a paradigm that supports the interaction created when talk is added to the reading-writing connection. The authors' work includes theoretical perspectives, models of application, and musings about assessment practices and their implications at home, at school, and in the curriculum at large. Especially helpful in all these chapters are the wonderful transcripts of learners engaged in envisioning their worlds, which provide an example of the kind of rich classroom talk that occurs when teachers give up the old directorial role and begin to model truly democratic discussions.

Andrew Wilkinson (1965) coined the word *oracy* to stress the importance of the language skills of listening and speaking. We are familiar with the view of literacy as an agent for empowerment. However, this book will implicitly and explicitly argue for the power of oracy to bring about change. The concept of universal entitlement to free speech to construct our lives has been a keystone in the search for a curriculum that strengthens the student to take an active place in society. There has been a particular exploration of the debate about what oral language is and its implications for curriculum. The authors of this work demonstrate that they are all committed to talk as the primary mode of learning, and they show that oracy in the curriculum can, and should, be a learner's opportunity to envision the possible.

## References

Bakhtin, M.M. (1981). *The dialogic imagination: Four essays* (C. Emerson, Trans.). In M. Holquist (Ed.). Austin, TX: University of Texas Press.

Barnes, D. (1976). *From communication to curriculum.* Harmondsworth, UK: Penguin.

Barnes, D., Britton, J., & Torbe, M. (1986). *Language, the learner and the school* (3rd ed.). Harmondsworth, UK: Penguin.

Mehan, H. (1979). *Learning lessons.* Cambridge, MA: Harvard University Press.

Vygotsky, L.S. (1962). *Thought and language* (E. Haufmann & G. Vakar, Trans.). Cambridge, MA: MIT Press.

Vygotsky, L.S. (1978). *Mind in society: The development of higher psychological processes.* (M. Cole, V.J. Steiner, S. Scribner, & E. Souberman, Eds. & Trans.). Boston: Harvard University Press. (Original work published 1934)

Wilkinson, A. (1965). *Spoken English.* Birmingham, UK: University of Birmingham Educational Review.

# Shaping Our Worlds: The Role of Oral Language in Children's Learning

*Patricia G. Smith*

Language has made possible man's progress from animality to civilization. But language has also inspired that sustained folly and that systematic, that genuinely diabolical wickedness that are no less characteristic of human behavior than are the language-inspired virtues of systematic forethought and sustained angelic benevolence. Language permits its users to pay attention to things, persons and events, even when the things and persons are absent and the events are not taking place. Language gives definition to our memories and, by translating experiences into symbols, converts the immediacy of craving or abhorrence, of hatred or love, into fixed principles of feeling and conduct. (Huxley, 1959, pp. 167–168 )

Language is a matter of people making signs to each other. This signing, or semiotic process, displays paradoxical aspects: It is both abstract and concrete, both fixed and developing. That is, many of the linguistic symbols and gestures that we use to communicate among ourselves have been codified into standard, abstract, stylized, and universally recognizable forms. In the process of using those symbols, individuals are constantly modifying their meanings, sounds, and shapes to suit their own particular purposes. And those modifications point to material and individual appearances, to the unique and individual character of their utterer—to that person's learning. Although thinking, knowing, and understanding are important steps in a progressive learning process, their operation appears, like talk, to be circular and recursive, and their ultimate outcomes are often not completely obvious.

Speech is the expression of self. We bring all that we are for others to see when we speak. The words are our connection to each other and to all of those that have gone before. We need to make these connections to live freely knowing that our words count in our worlds.

By talking, by exchanging and comparing feelings, thoughts and impressions in language, students learn not only to understand each other but also to see their own interpretations of events in contrast to ways others see them. Talk can be explained as a sign pointing to growing awareness of one's relationship to and distinction from others, as a sign of understanding one's own nature and position, and as a sign of self-understanding.

# Thought and Language: Theoretical Perspectives

Perhaps these ideas may be explained by considering the arguments of Vygotsky (1987) and Bakhtin (1981). Vygotsky's early 20th century modernist work may seem outdated to the poststructuralist reader. The poststucturalist revels in fragments, while Kozulin (1990) showed that Vygotsky is interested in the parts that make up the whole, like a mosaic. But he worked quickly, over 10 years, and his work often became postmodern in practice, in form, and in many of its conclusions as it crossed and recrossed disciplinary and conceptual borders. Art history, anthropology, linguistics, language education and, in fact, any revelation of the mind at work are used for a holistic purpose (Vygotsky 1971; 1978).

One of the pervasive themes that runs through Vygotsky's work is the unity and diversity of human consciousness. He attempts to explain human consciousness in all its variety. Language, and sign systems generally, become central because signification is the key process of consciousness. Wertsch (1991) argues that Vygotsky never reduces consciousness to inner speech nor solely to verbal or cognitive processes. Consciousness clearly involves affect and sensation, both of which are always woven into words that themselves primarily are means for talking about signs.

The structures of speech and thought are not mirror images of each other—Vygotsky (1978) is not saying that social relations and thinking are identical; rather he argues that they form a unity, inextricably related and bound with each other. Our inner world is connected with our outer world and our individuality is predicated on our membership in a community (and vice versa). Social relations are transformed when they are internalized by the individual who to a great extent decides what is important and why. The individual reconstructs and enfolds, or unfolds, the social semiotic accordingly. Inner speech is a kind of abstraction of speech activity, as speech activity is a kind of abstraction of a community experience or activity. So thought may be pushed and pulled into varying shapes as it turns into the speech that gives it expression, reality, and form.

This clarification deals with the false conclusion that if the mind is social, it necessarily cannot be individual and that Vygotsky views human beings as robots programmed to think in a certain way. This is disguised behaviorism inappropriately applied to the social realm, and Vygotsky (1978) vehemently denies such individual versus society dichotomies and resulting conclusions. Also, the distinction that is made between identity and unity refutes the proposition that we think only in words or in language. Clearly this is not the case although one component of our mental world is verbal. Vygotsky does not identify consciousness or thinking with language, and even if he did, he does not identify internal language with external language. For Vygotsky, inner speech and outer speech are quite different and distinct things. They are related but not identical (Vygotsky 1962; 1987).

This can be explained more fully if we understand that inner speech is critical to the whole idea of thought. Vygotsky (1962) in the final chapter of *Thought and Language* describes thinking developing into words through several intermediate phases including imaging, inner speech, inner speaking, and speech. Inner speech is the constantly shifting amalgamation of words and images, voices and tones, that seem to be at the heart of consciousness as all individuals experience it. Yet this private speech is also a social product, the result of our experiences. Vygotsky argues that inner speech first seems to be shortened and compressed into more compact units, and that these fused units take on new meanings and senses in addition to their earlier, relatively separate ones and flow out in extremely context-dependent ways. Because of this, speech is speeded up when it enters the realm of inner speech, thus allowing more information to be processed before the constraints of short-term memory begin to be felt.

M.M. Bakhtin has been especially clear about the need to see language, literature, and thinking in constant movement. This view of language complements Vygotsky's view of consciousness. Bakhtin and his followers disdain the simplistic sender-receiver models that have traditionally dominated thinking about language. They find the essence of language to be dialogue. Volosinov (1973) (some say a pseudonym for Bakhtin himself) argues that dialogue is the basis of inner speech. Bakhtin (1986) denies the proposition that language is a static, monolithic, arbitrary, and conventional matching of sign to referent or signifier to signified—an instrument used primarily for the sending and receiving of messages among individuals. He sees language as a multivoiced plurality—even the language that seems the most unified and monologic—which constitutes the language of our own utterances and our individual thoughts. We are constantly in dialogic conflict. This explanation seems very like Vygotsky's inner speaking.

## Talking It Through: The Role of Narrative Discourse

The inner speech we use is learned in social interaction. We use the experiences of such discourse to handle our experience narratively in our minds. It would be unusual to find people who would not admit to telling stories in their heads. We daydream and dream in narratives. No one seems to take much notice of this but narrative is the fundamental way in which the mind works, according to Bakhtin (1986).

Conversations are socially shared experiences. Roles are acted out as the teller uses his or her voice to make the characters real and the engaged listener imaginatively empathizes and responds. This narrative behavior can be attributed to the form existing in our natural worlds. We speak in realistic texts because life exists in episodes and events that are bound by causality. However, order exists in our discourse because we make it exist; it is intertextual, not inherent. The narrative is realistic because we understand the conventions of producing realistic texts and we are persuaded. Stories convince us, not because they are lifelike but because they are storylike. Narratives should not be judged by comparing them to life but by how they shape knowledge and help the listener "know."

Rosen (1982) proposes that a view of narrative that does not take account of its use of argument or any kind of conversation is bound to be an impoverished view. He argues that narrative discourse is essentially dialogic. This fits with Bakhtin's proposition that argument is an integral part of narrative discourse—the very discourse we have been discussing when considering the nature of conversation.

Carol Fox (1993), who has helped us learn much about children's storytelling, describes discourse as the language used by storytellers to engage the attention of listeners. She also elaborates on the communicative, reciprocal interaction of storytelling. The storyteller, often using elaborate and subtle discourse, claims a collaborator. Labov (1972) contends that the narrator's attitudes and feelings, without which we would only have a list of events, act as an evaluation aimed at obtaining response from the collaborator. Labov claims that "Evaluative devices say to us: this was terrifying, dangerous, weird, wild, crazy; or even amusing, hilarious, wonderful, more generally that it was strange, uncommon or unusual—that is, worth reporting" (p. 371). His narrative syntax is a model of story structure that allows for descriptions of storytelling competencies in specific cultures and social settings.

Meek (1991) focuses on the primacy of narrative in literacy learning. Drawing from the work of poststructuralists such as Genette and Barthes, she shows that even young children learn about highly complex structures when they are read well-crafted books. It is in their oral stories that we can see what has been learned because the structures emerge without the children's conscious forethought. They have learned the many possibilities of how texts can be read by the listener.

It is important to see that what is being described here is oral narrative, a performance reliant upon successful participation skills that must be practiced. Everyday conversations have complex functions and the potential for sophisticated learning and discovery. In other words, the composition of even the simplest narrative is very complex, as the following discussion between Casey's aunt Kerry and a friend, Megan, shows.

| Kerry: | I went to Casey's birthday party yesterday. I wasn't so keen to go. The thought of 12 five-year-olds in the garden was a bit much. She wanted a dress-up party so everyone was asked to come for a circus party. In the end I was running late and I had to buy her some books and a read-along tape. She loves Winnie the Pooh so I luckily found a tape she didn't have. I got the new Mem Fox book about bears that Anne told us about the other day. |
|---|---|
| Megan: | Great! I haven't.... |
| Kerry: | They had signed copies. |
| Megan: | Signed copies? |
| Kerry: | True! I couldn't believe my luck. I got a copy for myself, too. They have some left if you want one. |

The flow of talk here seems continuous and unstoppable, but a story has been constructed because the speaker has sequenced events with a beginning leading to the real purpose—the unexpected signed copy. The characters and setting have been introduced. The speaker has been selecting and discarding irrelevancies until finally the purpose is achieved—the sharing of the unexpected pleasure of an autographed copy of the new book. We can see that the speaker is trying hard to win and keep the attention of the audience. As Todorov (1977) explains,

> There is no "primitive narrative." No narrative is natural; a choice and construction will always preside over its appearance; narrative is a discourse not a series of events. There exists no "proper" narratives as opposed to "figurative" ones…all narratives are figurative. (p. 55)

It follows that conversation—spontaneous oral narrative—is an active meaning-making process. The conversationalists are constantly renewing the tactics and strategies learned in previous conversations.

## Developing Skills Through Oral Language

Andrew Wilkinson (1965) coined the word *oracy* in the 1960s in the United Kingdom, and it is a pity that this term is not used more widely as the role of talk in learning and its importance in shaping thought, internalizing concepts, developing arguments, and its interplay with other language modes is being explored in classrooms. When we talk of oracy in classrooms it becomes as important as literacy. What does it mean to teach and learn oracy? What are the purposes of talk in classrooms? The discussion so far could be simplified by arguing that language is learned through its use for three main purposes:

- learning about and developing an understanding of society
- negotiating with others meaning, understanding, and relationships
- making and interpreting performance

Although it is difficult—even undesirable—to compartmentalize language functions, it is nevertheless helpful if one or the other of these three purposes is used as a focus in curriculum. These categories reflect Halliday's (1978) ideas about the functions of language. The basic *experiential structure* tells us who is doing what to whom or what. The second type of meaning that Halliday refers to is *interpersonal meaning*, which is realized through the register of tenor. The third type of meaning, *textual meaning*, refers to how the clause is structured as a message. The theme develops from one message to the next using grammar as a tool. Halliday argues that by taking interpersonal and textual meanings into account the importance of different genres meaning very different things becomes apparent. The context of culture underpins this purposeful language as does the context of situation by setting the register of field, mode, and tenor. Students learn the grammar of speech, which is different from that of writing, and through debate, conversation, and argument they become critical learners who have mastered the speech genres of their culture.

Language is not merely a tool for describing what one already knows. It is a pervasive process through which we learn about our world and develop our creative and problem-solving skills. We do this by embodying and elaborating personally useable concepts in the form of words, tones of voice, and sentence structures. Given its flexibility and the opportunities it presents for efficiently transforming learning experiences into cognitive structures, talking is a particularly good way of developing and extending out understandings through inquiry. Talk enables the social construction of meaning as students are impelled to use, explain, discuss, and ask questions about the topics they are studying in all areas of the curriculum.

Talking is an essential way of exploring ideas; researching problems; negotiating relationships, understandings, and agreements; and reaching decisions among groups of people. It is important for students to get regular experience in using talk in small-group situations so they develop the ability to discuss issues that are important to them with confidence and sensitivity. Through experience in talking with others, students may learn to share ideas, develop new insights, dispel misunderstandings and misconceptions, and discover ways of building relationships and taking action that promote the well-being of both the individual and the group.

Many of the activities that go on in a modern society are profoundly influenced by the way that oral language is used in the processes of public decision-making, of buying and selling, of disseminating news and information, and of entertaining public audiences. Even the ability of individuals to make their voices, ideas, and opinions heard in semipublic situations has consequences both for the individuals concerned and for society in general. It is necessary for students to develop a critical understanding of the power and effects of oral language as it is used in situations of public performance. It is equally necessary for students to develop their ability to make public statements of their own. Through the development of their critical and creative oral language capacities students prepare to participate actively in society.

This concern about empowerment of learners seems to naturally relate to the work of Paolo Freire, the Brazilian educator and philosopher who was, like Bakhtin, interested in a dialogic methodology. Freire (1973) was particularly concerned with enabling poor workers to become literate so that they would step toward decision making and power sharing and become critical thinkers. He found that many Brazilian nonliterates believed that there was no way to change their lives because all that happened was due to God's will or to fate. They did not know the difference between nature and culture, that they had control over their lives. Like Vygotsky, Freire knew that the difference between humans and animals is language. He had an artist friend develop a series of 10 pictures that were designed to encourage the participants, in discussion, to consider complex issues to do with their culture. They learned they could, as a group, develop critical consciousness by looking at themselves and reflecting on their activities, all before they began learning to read and write.

Freire (1970) was concerned because many teachers see their job as transmitting predetermined knowledge or skills that the students need to meet the demands of society. He called this view the "banking model of education" (p. 53), which encourages passivity rather than critical thinking. Freire wanted problem-posing to be central to learning. He envisaged students entering into dialogue with their teachers and each other to develop a critical view of their reality, working through and confronting issues of significance in their lives. Freire's view, which acknowledges the connection between language used critically and awareness of self in social relations, fits well with Vygotsky's developmental psychology. Both emphasize the importance of the interaction between people and social experience in the move from inner speech to speaking.

## Classroom Dialogue

Having discussed a theory of dialogue, it should be considered how this theory might play out in the practice of the classroom. Barnes, Britton, and Rosen (1969) published the seminal *Language, The Learner, and The School*, which contains extensive transcripts of teacher–pupil dialogue and group discussions. The conclusions drawn from these transcripts are still relevant today. In this study classroom dialogue was shown to be essentially a series of exchanges between the teacher and individual students, where teachers monopolized any commentary on the students' answers. Within this restricted form of dialogue, there was evident a huge gap between the language and conceptual frame of the teacher and that of the students.

Labov and Fanshel (1997) point out that

> Conversation is not a chain of utterances but rather a matrix of utterances and actions bound together by a web of understandings and reactions.... We do not see conversation as a linguistic form. We have come to understand conversation as the means by which people deal with each other...to interpret to each other the significance of the actual and potential events that surround them and to draw the consequences. (p. 30)

Dixon (1974) suggested that teachers could learn to improve their dialogue with students by following these guidelines:

> Try to understand how assumed (or negotiated) rights, desires, obligations, abilities, and needs structure a social exchange.

> Recognise that understanding has to reach well beyond the sentence or utterance, moving through provisional (because open-ended) expansions to underlying propositions that may well be tacit.

> Read the interplay of speech acts, especially for their combined, progressive effect on interpreting the significance of events.

> Bear in mind varying levels of abstraction in the interpretation of what is said and done.

> Include the participants' retrospective interpretation as evidence.

> Do not expect a one-to-one relation of form and speech act, or of utterances and any overall expansion of what's said.

Underlying these understandings of spoken language is the implicit belief that spoken language in the classroom should be developed in a context of living issues, of critical inquiry into how the world is and not of random topics that encourage talk for talk's sake. This implies that the context for curriculum should be the whole curriculum. Barnes (1982) argued that the purpose of classroom talk should be to learn to understand and influence the world through speech, not to develop decontextualized speech skills that may prove to be a chimera. Teachers, interested in how their students could learn to read their worlds critically, should give them opportunities to argue for their rights, to persuade, to canvas opinions, to present a case, to plan with others to attack a problem or to explain a matter on which they have expert knowledge.

What is needed is not a new subject to teach (oracy) but a review of teaching in all disciplines. Teachers should stress the uses of spoken language as a tool for inquiry, discussion, and other critical inquiry activities as students seek to understand the world in which they live and to take an active role in it. Oracy should be a tool for students to use for critical understanding and action.

# Assessment of Oral Language

By showing and exchanging our understanding in the form of words and gestures, we show signs of ourselves and our learning to others, and we develop mutual agreements about the meanings of certain patterns of symbolic behavior. Spoken words can be assessed as signs pointing to social understandings among people, but great care, intelligence, and compassion must be exercised in this form of assessment. The act of talking, once understood as an act of self-revelation, brings forth a train of consequences and manipulative possibilities affecting one's status in the eyes of others as well as one's own self-esteem. For this reason, the situation in which oral language is assessed should be arranged scrupulously so that the student's own words are not turned against him or her.

Any object or symbol may arouse any number of meanings, memories, images, ideas, or feelings in the minds of its beholders. For example, Ψ could suggest a bird's foot, a fleur-de-lis, the dendrites of a nerve ending, or the confluence of three watercourses. Within the context of this book, the symbol is meant to suggest the ambiguity of linguistic signs. The signs presented by a teacher, though logically arranged, may seem incomprehensible to students. Likewise, the signs made by the students may seem meaningless unless the teacher is familiar with the contexts in which the students have learned to use them. Words should constitute a starting point for further learning and for the consolidation of caring relationships among the members of the learning community. Then, some fair assessment can occur.

The main issue facing teachers and students alike is the remote and learning-restrictive nature of traditional schooling. The traditional schooling situation, being removed and isolated from most of the natural activities of life, presents serious difficulties to teachers who wish to engage and activate the natural creative and learning powers of their students. Hence the futility of much of the well-meant advice designed to structure the learning situation so that its requirements naturally impel students to use and develop language to address real and meaningful tasks, issues, and problems. Given this state of affairs, the teacher has a choice. He or she must decide whether to regard the assessment of oral language as an opportunity to judge the correctness of student understandings, or to see both teaching and assessment as invitations to converse with students in an insightful way. The teacher must work to understand the students' world in the way that they do, so as to join and enlarge both teacher and student learning by mutually creating a third dimension of comradely talk.

Oral language, like written language, can be made to proceed in linear fashion from an introductory proposition stating the first principle, through a series of logically sequenced argumentative steps, to a seemingly inevitable conclusion deliberately placed at the end of what appears to be a straight track.

However, it is more common for natural discourse to emanate in circular patterns of exploratory thought, with many digressions and impressions sketched along the way. For this reason, listening to and assessing talk may be more appropriately approached as one would in examining a set of pictures that are subject to many interpretations, with much guessing and questioning about meanings.

Traditional assessment usually requires the study of visual symbols—graphic artifacts that stay in place and give the assessor time to grasp them. Yet these visual symbols only commemorate, in stylized form, one part of a linguistically and educationally meaningful event; they are not of themselves the event itself. It is not surprising that traditional assessment, like traditional curriculum, often works against the natural principles by which language and learning are developed. The most basic of these principles is that spoken language is the primary form of language and the primary mode of learning is developed in ongoing interaction (talk) with others—not in mute seclusion. It follows that assessment practices need to be mindful of cultural diversity. Yetta Goodman (1991) gives a timely warning about the need to consider language differences in the areas of dialect and second language learning:

> Too many children have been hurt in the past because of lack of knowledge about language differences. Not only teachers but the makers and curriculum builders often produce materials that reflect myths and understandings.... Attitudes such as "these children have no language" or "bilingualism confuses children" are still too prevalent. (p. 24)

It is perhaps the most dangerous myth of all to believe, as Labov (1972) also argues, that verbally deprived children have no language, because this belief diverts attention from the real defects of our educational system to imaginary defects of the child.

Some linguists and writers have realized that what we assess as factual or logical or reasonably argued depends on the culture and social class within which we are speaking. This insight has powerful implications for modern, democratic, and multicultural education. It implies that we should beware of using the dialect preferences of students as measures of their intelligence and ability to think and to argue. It means that we should assess our language curriculum to ensure that it realizes an overall aim of helping students learn to adapt and extend their use of talk so that they become able to function in a broader range of situations. It points out the fallacy of the language curriculum that tries to fit students with a standardized speech that, in fact, does not suit all purposes or all people on all occasions. In the words of Jean-Paul Sartre (1988),

> [T]he fundamental error of strict stylists is that they see speech as a Zephyr that flows lightly over the surface of things, that touches without changing. They see the speaker as a mere Witness who sums up, in a word, his innocu-

ous observation. But, to speak is to act; whatever one names can thenceforth never be exactly the same again, it has lost its innocence. If you point out the behavior of an individual, you reveal it to him: He sees himself. And if, at the same time, you describe him in the presence of others, he perceives himself to be seen in the same instant as he sees himself; the furtive mannerism that he forgot even as he displayed it looms large, exists for all to see; his person is drawn into the light of objective consideration, it takes on new dimensions, he sees himself through your gunsights. After that, how can you expect him to go on as before? (pp. 12–13)

Unless we alter the function of assessment to match these principles and to match the apparent function of universal education—the promotion of the learning of all people—then we can expect to produce a curriculum mode suited mainly to a select minority of learners who can overcome the unnatural obstacles of silence, passivity, and isolation that traditional assessment throws in the way of most people's learning.

In sum, oral language is very fluid—the form of our language and the nature of our thoughts and understandings may change and develop quickly as we reshape our feelings and impressions in the form of spoken words and gestures. This kind of thought is at once individual and social. It should be assessed over periods of observing real dialogues in which students are genuinely moved to shape and reshape their feelings, thoughts, and language in response to ongoing and authentic interaction with alternate interpretations of meaningful events.

## Authentic Assessment

Taking all of the above into account, the bar for reaching an authentic assessment of oracy in schools is set very high. The two main obstacles are the unavoidably artificial setting for the simulation of a range of "real life" tasks, and deciding what growth in speaking and listening might mean. Criteria used for assessment, especially for detailed analytical marking, should not implicitly evoke educational ground rules of the past. Such criteria for speaking and listening import a prescriptive element into what is supposed to be a value-free, objective analysis. Often high ratings are given for students' readiness to use a literary model which shows a clear beginning, middle, and end; details the setting; and ascribes thoughts and purposes to the protagonist. It is questionable whether literary criteria such as this should be used in an oracy test.

Criteria for assessment must be explicit in order to ensure that students understand the knowledge which will be legitimated or rejected in the classroom. Consideration may, in the future, be given to having students negotiate the criteria and the assessment process. Criteria are usually developed by those who have insider knowledge. Students could be at least made aware of the criteria.

In the end though, authentic assessment implies context. There may be more scope for authenticity if teachers are able to assess in context. Teachers and students can jointly create contexts that will provide students with both a rationale for understanding and evaluating present activity and a strong foundation for future development. Assessment will then become a collaborative, negotiated process between teacher and student—an act by which they both become more critically aware of what is happening

## Setting a New Paradigm

We should be concerned with talk in classrooms. This first chapter has provided an overview of the field, attempting to highlight various aspects that will be developed in the chapters that follow. It attempts to shape the reader's thoughts in a dialogic exchange. It has argued that the concept of universal entitlement to use free, critical speech to construct our lives has been a keystone in the search for a curriculum that strengthens the student to take an active place in society. This chapter has particularly explored the debate about what oral language is and looked at implications for a curriculum that can and should be a learner's opportunity to envision the possible. The curriculum should serve as a metaphor for the lives learners want to live and the people they want to be (Harste, 1994). This view of curriculum has important implications for classroom teachers and their practice. We need to be able to support learners to imagine other ways of being in and with the world. Oral language assessment practices that encourage the individual's confidence of his or her worth to society have been particularly considered. Unity has been addressed in the exploration of the relationship of the individual and society, and as the focus of purpose in curriculum and assessment.

### References

Barnes, D., Britton, J., & Rosen, H. (1969). *Languge, the learner, and the school.* London: Penguin Books.

Barnes, D. (1982). Finding a context for talk. *Spoken English, 15,* 2.

Bakhtin, M.M. (1981). *The dialogic imagination: Four essays* (C. Emerson & M. Holquist, Trans. & Eds.). Austin, TX: University of Texas Press.

Bakhtin, M.M. (1986). *Speech genres and other late essays* (V.W. McGee, Trans.). In C. Emerson & M. Holquist (Eds.). Austin, TX: University of Texas Press.

Dixon, J. (1974). Processes of formulation in group discussion. *Educational Review, 26*(3) 241–250.

Fox, C. (1993). *At the very edge of the forest.* London: Cassell.

Freire, P. (1970). *Pedagogy of the oppressed.* New York: Herder & Herder.

Freire, P. (1973). *Education for critical consciousness.* New York: Herder & Herder.

Genette, G. (1980). *Narrative discourse: An essay in method* (J.E. Lewis, Trans.). Ithaca, NY: Cornell University Press.

Goodman, Y. (1991). Kidwatching: Observing children in the classroom. In D. Booth & C. Thornley-Hall (Eds.), *The talk curriculum* (p. 25). Melbourne, Australia: Australian Reading Association.

Halliday, M.A.K. (1978). *Language as social semiotic: The social interpretation of language and meaning*. London: Edward Arnold.

Harste, J.C. (1994). Literacy as curricular conversations about knowledge, inquiry, and morality. In R.B. Ruddell, M.R. Ruddell, & H. Singer (Eds.), *Theoretical models and processes in reading* (4th ed., pp. 1220–1242). Newark, DE: International Reading Association

Huxley, A. (1958). Education for freedom. In *Brave new world revisited*. London: Chatto & Windus.

Kozulin, A. (1990). *Vygotsky's psychology: A biography of ideas*. Cambridge, MA: Harvard University Press.

Labov, W. (1972). *Sociolinguistic patterns*. Philadelphia: University of Pennsylvania Press.

Labov, W., & Fanshel, D. (1977). *Therapeutic discourse*. New York: Academic Press.

Meek, M. (1991). *On being literate*. London: The Bodley Head.

Rosen, H. (1982). The importance of story. *Language Arts, 63*(3) 226–237.

Sartre, J-P. (1988). *What is literature and other essays*. (J. Mehlman, Trans.). Boston: Harvard University Press.

Scribner, S. (1985). Vygotsky's uses of history. In J. Wertsch (Ed.), *Culture, communication and cognition: Vygotskian perspectives*. Cambridge, MA: Cambridge University Press.

Todorov, T. (1977). *The poetics of prose*. Oxford, UK: Basil Blackwell.

Volosinov, V. (1973). *Marxism and the philosophy of language*. Boston: Harvard University Press.

Vygotsky, L.S. (1962). *Thought and language* (E. Haufmann & G. Vakar, Trans.). Cambridge, MA: MIT Press.

Vygotsky, L.S. (1971). *The psychology of art*. Cambridge, MA: MIT Press.

Vygotsky, L.S. (1978). *Mind in society: The development of higher psychological processes*. (M. Cole, V.J. Steiner, S. Scribner, & E. Souberman, Eds. & Trans.). Boston: Harvard University Press. (Original work published 1934)

Vygotsky, L.S. (1987). *Thinking and speech* (N. Minich, Trans.). New York: Plenum.

Wertsch, J. (1991). *Voices of the mind*. Hertfordshire, UK: Harvester Wheatsheaf.

Wilkinson, A. (1965). *Spoken English*. University of Birmingham, UK: Educational Review.

# Theoretical Tools for Talk

*Susan Hill*

This chapter begins with an excerpt from a collaborative classroom discussion. The teacher initiated the discussion by asking the students what they would do of they needed to get assistance in the community. In the excerpt, the six students engage in a discussion about safety houses where opinions differ and ideas are negotiated.

| | |
|---|---|
| Sam: | I'd like I'd go to like the nearest house. |
| Rina: | The nearest house or safety house? |
| Sam: | Yeah, a safety house. |
| Vin: | Run to run to the nearest house. |
| Cass: | Safety house? Or nearest house? |
| Rina: | Safety house. |
| Cass: | Nearest safety house. |
| Jo: | Yeah, but supposing there's not a safety house around? |
| Rina: | Yeah, they're all around. I know where one is. |
| Vin: | I don't. |
| Fred: | I do. |
| Cass: | The school! The school is a safety house. |

(Bills, Lucas, & Cormack, 1998, p. 140)

The students in this discussion are learning through talk, and knowledge comes into being through the conversation itself as students build understanding about what a safety house is.

This chapter explores different theories and assumptions about talk. The theories are viewed as tools that shed light on different ways to understand talk. I have taken the view that no one theory can be all things to all educators and that admitting to holding an incomplete theory of how children learn can promote dynamic and ongoing inquiry into the complexity of how children learn to speak and listen.

I have taken a wide lens to explore talk in this chapter, but this does not deny the importance of focusing on technical skills or the cognitive aspects of spoken language; it understands these elements as they are encapsulated within cultural wholes. This approach allows for various theories to be used as tools with inherent advantages and disadvantages. This wide lens is based on Foucault's (1980) idea that working from one particular theoretical position with its particular process and discourse is not bad in itself, but that everything is dangerous if we cannot think and understand outside the frames and rules of one discursive position.

First, I describe five important theoretical perspectives on talk (based on Crawford, 1995); outline important ideas in each theory; and raise issues, pose questions, and suggest gaps in each view (see Table 1). Second, I explore two additional theories to highlight the complexity of speech differences between students at home and at school, and student and teacher interactions in school.

**TABLE 1**
**Theoretical perspectives**

|  | MATURATION | BEHAVIORAL | DEVELOPMENTAL PSYCHOLOGY | SOCIAL CONSTRUCTIVIST | CRITICAL |
|---|---|---|---|---|---|
| DRIVING THEORIES | Maturationism | Behaviorism | Cognitive and developmental psychology | Sociopsycho-linguistics, Cultural anthropology | Critical and feminist theories |
| DOMINANT RESEARCH PARADIGMS | Observation | Empirical-analytical | Symbolic | Symbolic | Critical |
| MAJOR THEORISTS | Froebel Gesell | Thorndike | Piaget | Vygotsky | Freire |
| GOALS | Give children time to mature and develop knowledge of self. | Direct instruction in the elements of speaking, listening, and interaction. | Support children in their cognitive construction of language. | Support children in their social construction of language. | Identify and change the sociopolitical power relationship. |

# Maturation Perspective

In a maturationist perspective all children are considered to pass through a series of invariant stages that cannot be hurried. Maturation occurs as a result of a biological process of neural ripening, similar to ripening fruit or blossoming flowers (Gesell, 1925). In this approach it is thought that nature must take its course and damage can be done if children are hurried too quickly. Speaking and listening are viewed as natural parts of development that are best left to grow unencumbered and uninterrupted by explicit teaching or intervention by the teacher.

The maturationist view can be criticized as a romantic, idealized view of the lives of many children. Linked to this is a worrying concept that language is genetically predetermined and that what is in the child at birth merely needs to be left to grow. The ideal world in this view often is a privileged one where all people have their genetically predeterminied place and this place is not questioned. Even though the idea of waiting for children to mature can be viewed as a little optimistic and dated, there are echoes of this perspective in the discourse of educators today when educators say things like "Give the child more time to develop," "Don't rush them," and "Children take their own time."

# Behavioral Perspective

In a behavioral perspective, rather than letting nature take its course, nurturing in the form of direct instruction takes precedence. Children must be taught how to speak and listen and their spoken language improves if systematic direct instruction is provided. Speaking and listening can be broken down into a series of isolated skills that can be arranged into a hierarchy. In this perspective the teaching of speech is an objective, scientific, and value-free process.

Programs based on behavioral assumptions were implemented in United States preschools in the 1960s when "President Johnson's war on poverty targeted the disparity that existed between those labeled as 'slum children' and those children who came from the dominant culture of middle class America" (Crawford, 1995, p. 73). One such program was DISTAR, a highly structured, focused, fast-paced, and skills-based direct-instruction program. In the DISTAR program the children were grouped according to ability and received small-group instruction during which they were required to provide a verbal group response to teacher queries (Spodek & Brown, 1993). DISTAR explicitly taught vocabulary, syntax, and interaction turns in repetitive drills. When educators talk of "fast-paced" learning and emphasize "time on task" there are echoes of this type of behaviorism.

One of the main criticisms of isolated skills and drills programs has to do with questions concerning how well the skills transfer to new learning situations. In addition, critics of this perspective ask what the students will learn, comprehend, and retain if the content has little to do with issues, problems, and emotions relating to their lives (Teale & Sulzby, 1986).

# Developmental Psychology Perspective

The developmental psychology perspective draws from the work of Piaget. This perspective states that all children move naturally through developmental stages in learning and that no stage can be skipped (Piaget, 1955). The process of acquiring oral language occurs within a sequence of stages throughout which teachers observe and monitor children's development. Age-related, developmentally appropriate practices guide the curriculum activities. Formal direct instruction, particularly the teaching of skills, is seen as inappropriate for young children as they must be encouraged to create their own conceptual frameworks for how language works. Educators who talk of a curriculum for children ages 4 and 5 or children ages 12 and 13 are often echoing stages of development based on developmental psychology.

This perspective discourages teacher-directed large-group instruction, preferring individualized child-initiated play or activity-based settings. The developmental principles reinforce the belief that generic patterns of language learning can be expected from all children regardless of their sociocultural experiences. If there is a deviation from the series of cognitive developmental stages, this is seen as a deficit. Learning is seen to happen best through active and meaningful engagement.

Developmental psychology works to produce a set of practices in which the teacher observes the child for "normal" development through ages and stages. Walkerdine (1984) suggests that such practices are normalizing in that they constitute a mode of observation and surveillance and a particular construction of children. The great diversity among children is discounted while a narrow band of behaviors is searched for and monitored. Walkerdine writes of how teachers once monitored the child for normal development:

> [T]he observation and monitoring of child development became a pedagogy in its own right because those understandings taken to underlie the acquisition of knowledge were presumed to be based on a "natural" foundation. The new notion of individualized pedagogy depended absolutely on the possibility of the observation and classification of normal development and the use of spontaneous learning. (1984, p. 177)

The discourse of developmental psychology has so dominated our experiences that we talk about ourselves and others as slow, advanced, mature, or weak in a particular domain, or ready for a particular experience (Cannella, 1997). As Cannella warns, the surveillance, measurement of what is judged as normal, and comparison of children (and other human beings) creates the conditions for social control—adult over child, middle class over the poor, and man over woman. It is difficult to conceive of these practices as any kind of pedagogy that could potentially "liberate" children or celebrate diversity and difference. Developmental psychology prompts teachers to focus on what children need to do next rather than what children can do in different contexts, and it can lead us to underestimate and miss out on different children's abilities.

## Social Constructivist Perspective

The social constructivist perspective draws primarily on the social interactionist theories of Vygotsky (1978). "For Vygotsky, children's cognitive development must be understood not only as taking place with social support in interaction with others, but also as involving the development of skills with sociohistorically developed tools that mediate intellectual activity," according to Rogoff (1990, p. 35). In a Vygotskian based curriculum, language is viewed as a cultural tool that acts to transform behavior as this behavior is internalized. Educators who comment on making the curriculum more relevant and meaningful to the students' worlds often echo social constructivist views. (See Chapter 1 for further discussion on Vygotsky's social contructivist views.)

Social constructivists suggest that children are competent and capable users of oral and written language. Children purposefully learn and make sense of the complex semiotic signs and symbols of their culture. This meaning-making or sense-making process in the young child is no different from the processes engaged in by older children and adults and there is no set of universal, invariant developmental stages. The differences between the processes of younger and more proficient language users is a matter of sophistication, practice, and experience, not a particular stage of psychological development. The activities of even very young children are reflective of their culture and are characterized by both purposefulness and intentionally (Crawford, 1995).

Social contructivists stress the importance of the teacher scaffolding learning for children. This scaffolding can mean that the teacher repeats or rephrases children's spoken language to model correct usage in different situations. In regard to modeling correct language usage, Cannella (1997) points out that social constructivists may unconsciously perpetuate the cultural capital of particular power groups by stressing that their own form of communication is to be used because it is superior to all others. In addition, social constructivism—like developmental psychology—runs the risk of imposing a discovery-based, problem-solving approach on all children. Success in discovery-based learning may depend on the availability of materials and particular resources at home. In addition, classrooms all over the world are colonized to be constructed in ways that are consistent with Western middle-class values.

# Critical Perspective

The critical perspective is similar to that of the social constructivist theorists except that the critical perspective acknowledges that the power bases within different sociopolitical contexts are not equal (Freire, 1970). This view contends that social practices are set up to meet the interests and help maintain the privileged positions of those within the dominant culture. Critical perspectives claim that the interests of the dominant culture are accepted more readily and have more influence than any minority interests that may seek to disrupt the existing hierarchical power relationships. These perspectives are therefore concerned with change and social action.

Critical perspectives view cultural and social identities as complex. Factors such as ethnicity, gender, religion, socioeconomic status, family education levels, and sociopolitical status all intertwine to result in individual cultural identities. For example, a female Vietnamese student whose parents graduated from high school will have a different sociocultural identity than a female Vietnamese student whose parents did not attend formal schooling.

In this view, like in the social constructivist view, most young children learn before formal schooling begins how to conduct themselves in complex literacy events in which there are different rules for participating in conversation. These events are connected intimately to the learning of community values, ideologies, and "namings" of the social and natural world. They are also a means for establishing identity and playing out age, gender, and authority relations with caregivers (Luke, 1993).

In a critical perspective, language education involves issues of social justice, ethnicity, social status, and gender. Gender, social status, and ethnicity all intertwine to create a "sociocultural identity kit" (Hill, 1997), and language is a powerful source of identity formation. Children arrive at school with different identity kits that are acquired from enculturation into the community's social and cultural practices. This "kit" is acquired through social interaction with people who have already mastered this way of being and way of learning within the social and cultural community. A home-based primary discourse that is similar to the secondary discourse of school can facilitate learning, but as Gee (1987) notes,

> Children from non-mainstream homes often do not get the opportunities to acquire dominant secondary discourses—including those concerned with the school—in their homes, due to their parents lack of access to these discourses. At school they cannot practice what they haven't yet got and they are exposed mostly to a process of learning and not acquisition. Therefore, little acquisition goes on. (p. 9)

Simple teaching methods like skill and drill activities will not help children who have acquired a different sociocultural identity kit or way of being from that of the dominant school culture. Another critical view claims that

(J)udgements of deficiency, dysfunction, and irresponsibility are all culturally relative stances. They are made by educators who cannot or will not step outside of their ethnocentric world to attempt to see their students from another perspective. When one is a participating member of a sociocultural group in power, this may be an acceptable response to the failure of schools. It is not a moral one, though, or an effective one, and serves only to perpetuate the situation. (Purcell-Gates, 1995, pp. 186–187)

Within a critical perspective, effective education should start with what the community values. For example, at Swallowcliffe, a school in a community with long-term unemployment, the curriculum focuses on collaborative learning, communication skills, problem solving, and conflict resolution (Hill, 1997). The principal commented,

This community is not a print culture. It is an oral culture. Families watch, listen and get information and entertainment from TV. All families have TV, videos, some have Galaxy TV. They have computers, Nintendo. Some might buy the *Sunday Mail* newspaper once a week. Most don't go to the library. Few would read the school newsletter. Families watch infotainment like *House and Garden* magazine-style information shows. They don't need to read and write. For them there is not much purpose in reading and writing. The soaps provide drama and the kids after about grade five, live out the relationship dramas like the soaps they watch on TV. (Hill, 1997, p. 272)

The parents at Swallowcliffe asked the school to conduct a parent group skills and communication program because they saw that their children had developed powerful oral language and group process skills and they wanted to learn with their kids. When the parents learned more about spoken communication and group skills they decided that they wanted to set up a School Community Contact Group. For this group to work effectively further parent sessions were conducted on group communication processes such as brainstorming, questioning, and ways to give feedback to a group.

From a critical perspective this social action program was set up around issues of concern to the community such as the following:

- exploring critical social issues and community resources and knowledge
- finding out about parenting, with topics like managing behavior, antiharassment, health, and nutrition
- using oracy to explore their own lives and experiences
- setting up school community liaison groups
- talking and writing to the school and community council, addressing local issues that relate to schools and preschools

Working from this perspective involves starting with what people know and can do. To be effective, educators have to be highly trained professionals with sufficient resources and time to customize the curriculum.

# More Theoretical Tools

There are two more theoretical tools that contribute to understanding talk in the classroom. The theories of Foucault and Bourdieu can be used to reveal complex social dynamics at work in pedagogy. These sociological theories are particularly relevant to understanding how talking in school is expressed by different groups of young students. The theories are complex because they explore the dynamics operating within social interaction. They contrast to many linear models for explaining how power works because they stress the connections among various elements or factors within different social spaces or social events.

## *Tools to Explore Institutions*

To explore how institutions work we need to refer to the work of Foucault (1980). Foucault is useful for understanding how schools work to make some students successful and others less so. His discourse theory (1970, 1972) is more subtle than just naming or labeling the social and natural world. For Foucault, rather than the simple transmission of knowledge and power as a top-down, overt, coercive force, there is instead diffuse power in the discourses enacted in a multiplicity of texts and institutional practices in everyday sites.

Power exists in the relationships between people that are played out in various roles. Simple oppositional roles such as adult/child, teacher/student, husband/wife, employer/worker are not just linguistic categories. These categories have assumed relationships that provide a grid of identities (Foucault, 1972). Discourses make up practical grids of specification for diagramming, classifying, and categorizing the subject in the social world. These grids are put to work in institutions in ways that generate self-surveillance, wherein the subject internalizes the disciplinary and cultural gaze as his or her own. "The effect is one of self-colonization, in which the subject takes on responsibility for monitoring her or his morality, discourse, and body" (Luke, 1992, p. 111).

Central to the efficiency of schools is institutional regulation and control through systems of surveillance and moral regulation. This regulation and surveillance is inscribed at the heart of teaching and is inherent to it and increases its efficiency. For example in education, categories are created and used in everyday institutional practices in which labels such as learning disabled; top, middle, and bottom group; and "skills-deficit child" are constructed in everyday institutional discourse such as face to face interaction, report cards, and other official documents.

Foucault provides insights into how the everyday classroom organization, grouping patterns, management structures, language, and teaching practices largely taken for granted work to construct school success or failure for particular students.

### Tools to Explore Social Capital

Another theoretical tool is provided by the critical sociologist Bourdieu (1986), who uses an economic metaphor to grasp the idea that capital (such as social or cultural capital) is cashed in in various fields or situations for rewards. Bourdieu's (1986) notion of how capital works can be simplified in this equation: (habitus x capital) + field = practice.

To explain this equation further, we must examine its components. *Habitus* is a worldview that includes dispositions and aspirations and a whole range of ritual practices, discourses, sayings, and proverbs, all structured in concordance with the principles of the habitus. The habitus inculcates dispositions that instill principles that affect what communities and families do and think they are doing. Importantly, the habitus is a mediating construct, not a determining one.

*Capital* for Bourdieu can be economic, cultural, social, and symbolic. Cultural capital is culturally valued taste and consumption patterns, art, education, and forms of language. In talk for example, culturally valued taste and a sense of one's social position can influence the choice of picture books, the form of literary language, the decision to use or not use nursery rhymes, supermarket books, and student worksheets. Social capital refers to group membership: families, church groups, community groups, clubs, parties, networks, and school groups. Social capital relies on the possession of economic and cultural capital, and can be fully realized only if the practices of community life are taken up or accessed by the school, university, or government agency.

Within this sociological analysis, the *field* is an area where there is conflict and struggles for position. Positions are determined by the allocation of specific capital to actors who are located in the field. However, positions once attained can interact with the habitus to produce different postures that have an independent effect on the economics of "position taking" within the field.

In this way the dominant habitus is transformed into a form of cultural capital that the schools take for granted. Poor achievement for some groups and success for others occurs when those with the appropriate cultural capital are reinforced with success while others are not.

Individuals move across numerous cultural fields where different knowledges, skills, dispositions, social relations, and linguistic practices are valued differently. The capital or resources of an individual may be valued in the local community group but this capital may be in competition with institutional values. For example, a child who has been socialized to use a particular verbal uptake in the home community may find this is at odds with school practices unless it is converted or "cashed in" in some way.

The study *100 Children Go To School* (Hill, Comber, Louden, Reid, & Rivalland, 1998) suggests that the children most likely to benefit from informal opportunities to transform play into literate practices through pedagogical interventions are those children who are well-versed in how to display their literate competencies. These children attract the teacher's attention and they understand how to pick up on the teacher's involvement and instructional offers.

The following two excerpts are from case studies by Barbara Comber and Meridee Cuthill in *100 Children Go To School* (Hill et al, 1998). They show how two sets of children respond to pedagogic interventions. In the first text Tessa is playing with her friends. It is evident how easily Tessa and her friends connect to the pedagogic intervention of their teacher.

| | |
|---|---|
| Tessa: | We gotta put the wires in somewhere. <br> (Tessa role-plays the phone ringing then answers the phone.) |
| Tessa: | (explaining to Teacher) My house is going to be on fire. |
| Teacher: | Who is in your house? |
| Tessa: | Me, Sophie, and Julie. |
| Teacher: | How did the fire start? |
| Teacher: | What are you going to do? |
| Tessa: | Ring the firemen. |

(The teacher talks through with Tessa what she would have to do: *The emergency number is ___. The address is ___.*)

| | |
|---|---|
| Tessa: | (interjecting) Doesn't matter! |
| Teacher: | Yes it does! |
| Tessa: | What's an address? |
| Teacher: | The number, the street, the suburb. |
| Tessa: | 50 Georgiefire Street. |
| Teacher: | I'll get some paper so you can make a sign. (p. 122) |

Compare this with a group of boys in Comber's study who are playing an imaginary game with the blocks—and who take the play curriculum very seriously—and notice how the teacher's pedagogic offers are rejected as an intrusion.

| | |
|---|---|
| Teacher: | There seems to be a slight problem with the roof here. <br> What's holding the roof up? |
| Paul: | The fence (inaudible). |

| Teacher: | Where's the wind coming from? How does it get past the fence? |
|---|---|
| Paul: | It jumps. |
| Teacher: | Since when can cars jump? |
| Paul: | (inaudible) |
| Teacher: | So these are rather special cars then? (Paul nods and smiles and M joins them and listens. Alan continues to play to one side, silently rebuilding his structures until Teacher addresses him directly.) Does your black car have writing on it? (No response from Alan.) Did you get that yesterday for your birthday? |
| Alan: | A squiggly pen. |
| Teacher: | What does it look like? |
| Alan: | A pen. |
| Teacher: | What's different about it then? |

The boys smile at each other, realizing that Teacher doesn't understand about battery pens. Alan returns to his structures and starts to destroy them with his car. (p. 91)

The interactions described in the transcript show how the teacher's interventions are picked up and used differently by different students. This highlights the need for caution in creating universal views of how all children learn. It also highlights the need for teachers to reflect on the kind of talk used in teaching and learning, and the use of a flexible repertoire of possible teaching strategies. Considering the importance of speech for learning; talk should not remain unproblematized and nor should teacher-student interactions continue to be resilient to change (Freebody & Ludwig, 1998).

Although talk is fleeting and hard to monitor, it deserves far more attention as a vehicle for learning. When teaching interactions do not work educators have to think outside traditional, familiar perspectives and search for different theoretic tools for understanding and improving practice.

## Final Thoughts

There are many different perspectives on talking and learning. In the past, theory has tended to be polarized into debates such as nature versus nurture and direct instruction versus discovery through play. The challenge for educators, researchers, and the community is to widen debates, to rethink and restructure spoken language practices, and to promote creative approaches to connecting language learning at home and in school.

We need to question notions of one universal set of developmental stages in language learning and question any one-size-fits-all style of pedagogy. Creative and thoughtful educators are aware that there are echoes of many theoretical perspectives in their educational discourse. Being conscious of how different theoretical perspectives work to construct the student and the teacher can alert us to new educational possibilities. Holding a working but incomplete theory of how children learn is a healthy starting point for further work and ongoing inquiry.

## References

Bills, D., Lucas, N., & Cormack, P. (1998). What kind of school based activities allow students to demonstrate achievement of outcomes in talking and listening? In P. Cormack (Ed.), *Classroom perspectives on talk: A report on collaborative research with teachers* (pp. 123–166). Canberra, ACT: Commonwealth of Australia.

Bourdieu, P. (1986). *Distinction: A social critique of the judgment of taste.* London: Routledge.

Cannella, G. (1997). *Deconstructing early childhood education: Social justice and revolution.* New York: Peter Lang.

Crawford, P. (1995). Early literacy: Emerging perspectives. *Journal of Research in Childhood Education, 10*(1), 71–86.

Foucault, M. (1970). *The order of things: An archeology of the human sciences.* London: Tavistock.

Foucault, M. (1972). *The archaeology of knowledge.* London: Tavistock.

Foucault, M. (1980). *Power/knowledge: Selected interviews and other writings 1972–1977.* (C. Gordon, Ed. and C. Gordon, I. Marshall, J. Mepham, & K. Soper, Trans.). Sussex, UK: The Harvester Press.

Freebody, P., & Ludwig, C. (1998). *Talk and literacy in schools and homes: A summary of the study "Everyday literacy practices in and out of schools in low socioeconomic urban communities."* Canberra, ACT: Commonwealth of Australia.

Freire, P. (1970). *Pedagogy of the oppressed.* New York: Seabury.

Gee, J. (1987). *What is literacy?* Paper presented at the Marlman Foundation Conference on Families and Literacy. Cambridge, MA: Harvard Graduate School of Education.

Gesell, A. (1925). *The mental growth of the preschool child.* New York: Macmillan.

Hill, S., Comber, B., Louden, W., Rivalland, J., & Reid, J. (1998). *100 children go to school: Connections and disconnections in literacy development in the year prior to school and the first year of school.* Canberra, ACT: Commonwealth of Australia, Department of Employment Education Training and Youth Affairs.

Hill, S. (1997). Perspectives on early literacy and home–school connections. *Australian Journal of Language and Literacy, 20*(4), 263–279.

Luke, A. (1992). The body literate: Discourse and inscription in early literacy training. *Linguistics and Education, 4*, 107–129.

Luke, A. (1993). The social construction of literacy in the primary school. In L. Unsworth (Ed.), *Literacy learning and teaching: Language as social practice in the primary school* (pp. 3–53). Melbourne, Australia: Macmillan.

Piaget, J. (1955). *The language and thought of the child.* New York: Meridian Books.

Purcell-Gates, V. (1995). *Other people's words.* Cambridge MA: Harvard University Press.

Rogoff, B. (1990). *Apprenticeship in thinking: Cognitive development in social context.* New York: Oxford University Press.

Spodek, B., & Brown, P. (1993). Curriculum alternatives in early childhood education: A historical perspective. In B. Spodek (Ed.), *Handbook of research on the education of young children* (pp. 91–104). New York: Macmillan.

Teale, W.H., & Sulzby, E. (Eds.). (1986). *Emergent literacy: Writing and reading.* Norwood, NJ: Ablex.

Vygotsky, L.S. (1978). *Mind in society: The development of higher psychological processes.* (M. Cole, V.J. Steiner, S. Scribner, & E. Souberman, Eds. & Trans.). Boston: Harvard University Press. (Original work published 1934)

Walkerdine, V. (1984). Developmental psychology and the child-centred pedagogy: The insertion of Piaget into early education. In J. Henriques, W. Hollway, C. Urwin, C. Venn, & V. Walkerdine (Eds.), *Changing the subject: Psychology, social regulation and subjectivity* (pp. 153–202). London: Cambridge University Press.

## For Further Reading

Cope, B., & Kalantzis, M. (Eds.). (2000). *Multiliteracies: Literacy learning and the design of social futures.* Melbourne, Australia: Macmillan.

Lindfors, J. (1999). *Children's inquiry: Using language to make sense of the world.* New York: Teachers College Press.

# Talking to Think, Learn, and Teach

*Bridie Raban*

## What Is Language?

Language, both spoken and written, is at the heart of teaching and learning. We learn to speak, listen, read, and write to make things happen, to keep things in control, to find things out, to understand things better, to keep track of our thinking, and for many other reasons.

Language is so closely bound with all the things we do that it is sometimes difficult for us to separate it as an object of study—thinking about it apart from its practical functions. Language is a multilayered set of subsystems, each of which is rule-governed. The surface features are easy to discern; for instance, we are familiar with the sounds of our own language such as the pitch contours and relative volume.

The ways in which these surface features convey meaning along with vocabulary choices, sentence structures, and the shape we choose to give a particular piece of discourse are not arbitrary. These various aspects of language are related to each other in intricate, rule-governed ways. When we learn language we learn how to orchestrate and control these different layers and the relationships among them to achieve our own purposes.

The complexity of language and language learning, therefore, defies any simplistic description or linear developmental pathway. However, this does not mean that we have no control over its increasing sophistication during the early school years. We know that language is sensitive to audience, context, and purpose, and that by manipulating these variables systematically we can ensure that students gain opportunities to use their language in a variety of ways. Through these experiences, students' language will develop recursively and they will be able to think and learn in increasingly appropriate ways.

Language is

- multilayered and rule-governed;
- a complex interrelation of subsystems;

- sensitive to context, audience, and purpose; and
- recursively developed.

We learn language and we learn about language by using it for all the purposes in our daily lives. Indeed, the notion of purpose in talk is the motivating factor of language development. We use increasingly more specific and sophisticated language as we shape our ideas more accurately in order to successfully share our understandings and beliefs with others. By doing this, we frequently discover more about our own ideas and we can modify them as a result of the feedback we receive.

## Speaking and Listening

At the center of spoken language learning is the quality of interaction between speakers and listeners. We know the significance of young children's spoken initiations and the influence of conversations with more knowledgeable others throughout the early years. We know the value of "contingent" responses to these initiations. If the responses that listeners make to speakers are noncontingent, that is they bear no relationship to what has been heard, then the conversation will not go on at length and the purpose of the exchange will be lost.

Noncontingent responses, therefore, will not satisfy the communicative purposes of human interaction. When we listen, we actively listen to make sure that our responses are linked, that they are contingent or dependent on what has been said before. This means that listeners work just as hard as speakers in their efforts to make sense of the spoken realizations of others' worlds.

Contingent responses

- keep conversations flowing,
- indicate active listening,
- provide positive feedback,
- are emotionally satisfying,
- extend meaning, and
- achieve a clear purpose.

Using the terms *speaking* and *listening* can misleadingly imply that these activities are different. They are not. The processes that are relevant to both speaking and listening are the same. Speakers and listeners construct a shared meaning through their conversations by using language to make this happen and to ensure that it is happening successfully.

Listeners do not decode speech sounds and sequences of words first and then read off the meaning after this decoding. They predict and anticipate what the speaker is talking about in real time and check their understandings of the meanings to be shared by responding as a speaker themselves. Both speaking and listening are dynamic and interactive processes.

# Development of Speaking and Listening

Learning to talk is not only about learning to structure sentences, but about learning to engage with other people, to respond to what they say, and to influence what they think and do. By the time students start school at age 5, they have acquired a large amount of knowledge about language. They speak like others in their family and community with respect to accent and dialect, they have an extensive vocabulary, and they use language for a variety of purposes.

These new school entrants have control over most of the grammatical structures of their first language, although some aspects of grammatical learning will continue to take place throughout the years of schooling. Naturally, they have adopted the speech patterns of those around them and this may not be Standard English. Their vocabulary, pronunciation, and sentence structures may be nonstandard, even when English is their first language.

However, young children are surprisingly sophisticated language users, using language for a wide variety of purposes. They are able to speculate, predict, hypothesize, express emotions, and negotiate. They know how to adapt their language to that of others, talk about things not immediately present and they know how to engage others in conversations for their own benefit. Children entering school can use language to joke, tell stories, enjoy conversations for their own sake, and give instructions to achieve outcomes.

Nevertheless, as Clay (1998) makes clear, there are wide individual language variations. Children's competence is dependent on the experiences of the world they bring with them to school and the opportunities they have been offered to share and talk about these experiences with more knowledgeable others. It is difficult for 5-year-olds to put themselves in the position of their listeners. They can inappropriately assume that everyone knows what they know, and although this may be true in a close family context, away from that familiar group children need to learn to be far more explicit.

# Speaking and Listening at Home

Children experience many opportunities for talk at home. They conduct conversations with people they know and who know them. When children share so much in common with others they can make a large number of assumptions and their talk does not have to be specific in every detail. Young children are frequently engaged in conversations about the "here and now," a context that is shared by both speakers and listeners. This makes it possible to refer to things perfunctorily in the knowledge that the listener will understand what is going on.

Conversations in the home are also about social contact and much of this is nonspecific, with each partner taking turns to keep in touch and share feelings, points of view, and comments on current experience. This kind of conversation is good for creating and developing the social relationships that are important for everyday life and for learning both inside and outside the classroom.

Home talk

- provides a familiar audience,
- uses known patterns of discourse,
- contains short exchanges,
- achieves an immediate purpose,
- supports successful communication,
- consists of long exchanges, and
- is usually between child and adult or child and other age children.

We know from the work of Snow (1991) that young children who experience a range of different kinds of language during their early years at home will be better able to take advantage of the linguistic environment of the classroom. Young children who have had opportunities in the home to talk at some length about things that are not immediately present and to listen to language used for these decontextualized purposes, will be experiencing the beginnings of learning the language of school.

These decontextualized experiences of language can be encouraged by inviting young children to talk about their day with someone who did not share that time with them. They may reflect on their day as they get ready for sleep, listen to stories and tales about other peoples' experiences, explain something to someone else, or plan what to do tomorrow.

There are two critical elements that distinguish this kind of talk: It extends ideas beyond the immediate moment and it gives the speaker a longer turn. The listener will require additional information on the subject matter as the context will not be immediately obvious. Because of this required expansion this type of talk is called "extended discourse." Children with experiences of this kind of language at home will be better able to enter the culture of schooling, a culture that is predicated on developing thinking beyond the school walls.

Extended discourse

- provides for elaboration,
- encourages depth of understanding,
- accounts for needs of listener,

- achieves a deferred purpose,
- is intellectually satisfying,
- establishes links between ideas and experience, and
- fosters precision and articulation of thinking.

Extended discourse and decontextualized language are the hallmarks of school language and learning. Later learning from texts, across the curriculum, will be of this kind (see Pigdon & Woolley, 1992). During primary schooling, students will learn how to respond to texts and how to create texts for themselves, both spoken and written.

## Speaking and Listening at School

As Wells (1986) and others have indicated (Howe, 1989; Norman, 1992), children arrive in school as competent language users. Most will be confident conversationalists but there will be a time of adjustment while they learn about school organization and routines, how to take their turn with a large number of other students, and how to join the discourse of the classroom. Some will learn quickly that certain kinds of talk are more appropriate in school, but those kinds of talk may be unfamiliar to them.

Speaking and listening in school are primarily used to clarify understanding in order to learn and think (Wood, 1998). The Vygotskian relationships (1962; 1978) between thinking and spoken or written language are best demonstrated for students through the process of talk. Talk in the classroom is for refining our ideas and framing informed conclusions. Teachers and students hypothesize, summarize, compare, contrast, classify, and clarify through their classroom talk.

In any classroom, however, there will be children who have less experience with the language of school (Hannon, 1995). In these cases it is the responsibility of the teacher to create opportunities for students to recognize the different forms and purposes of language, and to instruct them in how to take part in and respond to the language of the classroom, as was illustrated by Reid, Forrestal, and Cook (1989).

Students such as those in Heath's study (1983) who are not familiar with classroom talk may be tentative at first, and may remain silent during their early days and weeks at school, mistakenly creating the impression that they do not understand what is going on. However, even adults who are confident and competent language users may react in this way when they find themselves in unfamiliar circumstances. Teachers need to be patient and not rush to inappropriate conclusions concerning students' capabilities. They can make these students feel valued and secure by providing support and encouraging feedback, and by planning experiences that will engage their enthusiasm and interest. Through these experiences, students gain confidence as speakers, listeners, and learners in school (Geekie, Cambourne & Fitzsimmons, 1999).

School talk

- provides an unfamiliar audience;
- uses unfamiliar patterns of discourse;
- requires listening at length;
- has a delayed pupose;
- does not always support successful communication;
- consists of many, brief exchanges; and
- is usually between the child and same age children.

## Teaching and Learning Speaking and Listening

Speaking and listening for learning is best taught by engaging students in these activities with a clear purpose and then providing the assistance they need (Cazden, 1988). The speaking and listening behaviors of teachers have a powerful influence on students, acting as a model for them as teachers talk with students about their work, how they want them to proceed with activities, and how they generate criteria for judging success.

In language learning, comprehension (listening) exceeds production (speaking). In new contexts, students listen and learn until they feel comfortable with particular ways of talking. They join in tentatively at first, feeling their way and welcoming positive feedback for their efforts. Speakers look for support and encouragement as they learn a new way of speaking and learn about this new discourse (Hughes & Westgate, 1998).

The route from already known ideas to new ideas involves the interactive use of language between teachers and students and between students and other students. This is the power of language in creating new knowledge and it is central to the processes of learning that take place in classrooms (Donaldson, 1978).

Although a wide range of thinking, speaking, and listening activity takes place in school, the real business of talk in the classroom is learning a language for learning (Geekie & Raban, 1993). This kind of talk incorporates strategies that promote interaction and collaboration to reach agreed upon purposes and outcomes. Teachers need to plan to carry these activities further and take students to the next stages of their thinking process: reflection, evaluation, drawing conclusions, and reviewing (Jones, 1996).

The expansion of learning into these new stages ensures that students experience using language to organize and refine ideas. The practical outcome of an activity is not necessarily the end of the intellectual activity; returning to an activity, preparing the outcomes for display, and reshaping the outcome for other purposes will provide additional consolidation. These processes and others give students opportunities to focus their language, to learn language that is crafted for particular purposes, and to transfer that learning to other situations.

# Types of Talk

Talking and engaging in interactive conversation comes so naturally and is so pervasive that it is sometimes difficult to focus on the kinds of talk being used in the classroom at different times for different purposes, and to develop aspects of classroom talk for specific learning activities. In classrooms, the major purpose of talk is for learning about the world while simultaneously learning about language itself, and learning how to learn. This purpose is revealed through students' increasing ability to ask questions, predict outcomes, grasp main ideas, and give and follow instructions.

Interactive conversations involve both speakers and listeners who take care to ensure that they understand what is being talked about. They use verbal and nonverbal behaviors to supply information on the process of their co-construction of meanings, and both take a responsibility for the meanings that are shared. As suggested by Wells (1980), this view of interaction gives speakers and listeners active roles.

## *Speaking as Process*

When we communicate with other people, whether it is to provide them with some information or to ask them about their concerns or their experiences, the person who initiates the speaking has an idea in her mind about an action, an event, and/or a set of circumstances. These ideas emerge from the model of the world that the speaker possesses, which has been formed through her personal experience as she has lived her life.

For each of us, the unique model of the world we draw from to join in conversations is personal and rich with meaning. No one has experienced the world in exactly the same way as anyone else. A speaker can never transmit information to a listener that will be understood in exactly the same way as the speaker conceptualizes that particular piece of information.

In addition, the speaker has to choose elements of language that are temporal and sequenced. Language is the most effective form of communication because of its immediacy and its satisfying emotional impact, it also forces speakers to select an ordered sequence of items that occur in rule-governed patterns. However, this sequence of language will not necessarily represent the sequence underlying the ideas.

The chosen elements of language need to be transformed into speech that has an arbitrary, although conventional, relationship to the underlying ideas. This becomes clear when we turn to foreign language programs as we switch through radio or television channels. If we come across a language we can neither speak nor understand, the speech sounds are incomprehensible, representing ideas that are inaccessible to us.

## Listening as Process

Even when a listener understands and speaks the same language as fluently as the speaker, the activity of listening is not as simple as working backward from the speech sounds themselves to unlock the underlying meanings. Listeners do not unravel speech by attending to the pattern of the words directly and then reaching beyond the language to the intended meanings of the speaker. If you have tried to transcribe a tape recording of speech you know how hard this is if you do not already know what the speaker is talking about.

This may sound paradoxical, but listeners make sense of language just like speakers by making use of their previous experience and knowledge of the world. Interpreting what speakers say requires the listener to have expectations about how the world works. Understanding a speaker is the result of constructing meaning by anticipating and predicting talk in the light of relevant aspects of the listener's model of the world. This model has been developed from speakers' own experiences and accumulated knowledge base.

There can never be any certainty that we share exactly the same meanings through conversations. We make informed responses on the basis of numerous verbal and nonverbal cues made available to us by the speaker. The fact that people do hold successful conversations means that for those of us born into similar communities and social contexts, we will share sufficient numbers of experiences to make ourselves easily understood.

However, in speech there are procedures for checking and restating intended meanings if misunderstandings are suspected, such as asking, Do you follow? Is that clear? and Do you see what I mean? In these ways, meanings and understandings between speakers and listeners are negotiated and renegotiated in light of the feedback each receives through successive turns. This is the dynamic activity of discourse that is primarily concerned with the interactive and constructive sense-making that occurs during purposeful interaction within a shared social context.

## Processes of Talk in School

There are clear implications here for our work with students in schools. Misunderstandings can occur at many points in the process. Teachers, as mature adults, and young students do not have similar experiences of the world. Students may not be as verbally adept in choosing just the right word or phrase, they may not speak the same language with any facility, or they may arrive in school from different speech communities with diverse expectations.

Because of these limitations on the active process of coconstructing meanings through speaking and listening, there are clear principles that need to be in the forefront of teachers' minds when they engage in conversations with their students.

Teachers should

- listen actively to what students are saying,
- invite students to say things again choosing different words,
- respond to students by reflecting on and extending the meanings as understood, and
- give students opportunities to extend their linguistic repertoire and their unique experiences of the world.

Social talk is concerned with people getting to know each other and as such does have a place in classroom settings. Through social talk, students learn about each other and how to get along with other people. Students are observed to often move in and out of social talk while doing something together that demands more actions than words. There is a natural need to communicate, and this kind of language provides a powerful motive, not only to speak, but to speak with clarity and precision so that the listener can attend closely to what is being said. Wanting to find out about something increases attention, and classrooms that provide authentic purposes for communicative talk will stimulate the need to share meanings among students, in small groups and with the teacher. Collaborating toward shared understandings is at the heart of learning.

Cognitive aspects of talk are revealed through different ways of thinking. Although young students are keen to acquire new skills and abilities, they also learn how to talk about them during this process. This happens more quickly when they are involved in setting the purposes for an activity, asking questions for themselves, inquiring, observing, recording, reflecting, reviewing, and evaluating. Placing students in situations that demand these ways of using language will enhance the quality of student learning.

Vygotsky has argued that the ability to talk and think is in the first instance social and only later becomes cognitive: "Human learning presupposes a specific social nature and a process by which children grow into the intellectual life of those around them" (1978, p. 32). This is why it is important to allow for all kinds of talk in classroom activities as students develop as learners. They need to learn not only to participate in activities but to engage in the meanings that are embedded within them. In this way all knowledge is actively reconstructed by each student for themselves.

Learning and the acquisition of language are intricately involved with each other. Because of this, the quality of student learning is dependent on, first, the nature of the language used and, second, the relationships among the participants.

# The Role of the Teacher

In the classroom, teachers have a primary role in deciding and dictating the kinds of talk that accompany various activities. Teachers' own talk acts as a model for students, and teachers can use this to demonstrate how talk achieves different purposes.

Teachers need to bear in mind

- the interactive nature of language and learning,
- the social and structural conventions of speaking and listening,
- the kinds of responses that extend and support student talk, and
- the need to provide students with a range of purposeful contexts for talk.

Students' language will vary with audience, context, and purpose, and teachers will need to provide for different opportunities that give students experience of these three dimensions both inside and outside their classroom. In eliciting responses from students, first respond to what students are talking about, and then respond by modeling forms of language that are appropriate for the purpose of the moment.

Teacher responses include the following strategies:

- Make a statement about what you think that might invite a rejoinder or disagreement.
- Invite elaboration and rewording.
- Let students know if you are not clear about what is said or how it is said.
- Encourage questions from students.
- Keep silent at strategic moments—this encourages others to speak.

By using a range of strategies such as these, teachers begin to put students' language under pressure. This means that students will find it necessary to move toward more precise and explanatory speech as they explore different ways of saying something that matters to someone who wants to listen.

Although students are offered these opportunities to construct and transform their meanings, correction of their speech may be reassuring for the teacher but is not effective for students' language learning. Surface features of talk are highly resistant to this form of feedback. Alternatively, teachers need to control the speaking and listening agenda at a much deeper level of intellectual demand.

Teachers need to plan for

- opportunities for talk,
- learning activities that will promote talk,

- their own intentions for the activity,
- the students' intentions,
- the context of the activity, and
- the talk outcomes.

Students use talk effectively and imaginatively to communicate with each other and with teachers and other adults. They do this to share what they know and think, and to learn what others know and think. The role of the teacher is crucial in this process. Teachers use talk to discover what students already know so that they can build links between new information and students' prior knowledge. Students make sense of new experiences by integrating past experience with new information and thereby transforming their knowledge base. They do not learn one thing and then another in any additive manner. The transformations that take place as a result of learning provide a fresh basis for new learning.

Through talk, teachers can

- find out what students already know,
- discover students' thinking processes through active listening,
- help students access past experiences relevant to new activities,
- develop and extend students' thinking by building bridges from known to new information,
- model successful strategies, and
- encourage, support, and scaffold through appropriate feedback.

## *Planned Intervention*

Joining in with student activities rather than merely organizing and supervising them gives teachers a genuine role and offers opportunities for scaffolding student learning as it takes place. This intervention can be facilitated through the techniques of demonstrating, scaffolding, questioning, and active listening.

**Demonstrating.** A significant resource for students' language learning is hearing the effective and successful demonstrations of language that their teachers provide. Teachers can talk students through an activity and in this way demonstrate out loud how they use what they already know to solve new problems. By using current knowledge as a point of contrast and comparison with new experiences, they can verbally show how they ask questions of themselves, speculate on possible outcomes, and describe events and activities. Teachers need to make it clear that they expect students to go through similar processes and use similar strategies while they are engaged in the activity of problem solving for themselves.

**Scaffolding.** Conversations between students and their teachers about something that engages the student's interest need to be shaped carefully to match and then extend that student's understandings. Experience of this kind of talk is called *scaffolding* (Bruner, 1983; Wood et al, 1976), and it is a powerful strategy for teachers supporting student learning. Approaches to literacy learning based on this strategy—guided reading (Fountas & Pinnell, 1996) and shared writing (Cloonan et al, 1998)—are examples of opportunities for students to develop their literacy skills and abilities. However, talk of this kind is equally powerful for supporting all kinds of learning across the curriculum.

**Questioning.** Frequently, teachers use the strategy of questioning for interrogation rather than for explanation and collaboration, and this can be intimidating for students, rendering them silent and confused. More profitably, teachers can develop a questioning technique that students can take over for themselves as they explore new material and promote problem-solving strategies. These kinds of questions extend an idea, challenge an assumption, or clarify explanations. By helping students ask Who? Why? What? When? How? Where? teachers can discover more easily what students already know, and they will be in a better position to support their students' learning of new knowledge.

**Active listening.** Active listening, as opposed to merely hearing, also includes the option of remaining silent. Teachers need to show that they are listening and also that they allow for tentativeness. This provides opportunities for students to find their own voice while they struggle with new meanings. This technique also supports and enables students to use new words and new expressions in their move toward new knowledge.

## Using the SAID Framework

Frameworks can be helpful reminders for teachers when they are planning their classroom talk for specific instructional purposes. They will also use talk to organize the students and to manage activities, but when they are engaging students' minds for learning their talk will need a special focus and framework that students themselves can follow when reviewing or sharing their own work with others. A valuable framework for talk in the classroom is encompassed by the acronym SAID:

### Stimulate

introduces an activity

**Articulate**

> identifies the focus of discussion
>
> states clear goals

**Integrate**

> links new to previous knowledge

**Demonstrate**

> illustrates new knowledge in action

During the literacy teaching program, for instance, teachers can use this framework across a number of teaching approaches as illustrated by Essex and Raban (2000). These can include language experience, shared reading and writing, guided reading and writing, interactive and modeled writing, and reading aloud to students from across the curriculum. An example of the SAID framework in relation to one of these approaches is illustrated below. It gives a sense of how teacher talk in the classroom around the *language experience* teaching approach (Holdaway, 1979) can offer a focus for the talk of both teachers and students.

**Stimulate.** Engage students in thinking about what they want to record in writing. This writing may emerge out of an activity that has already taken place or is planned in the future. Through conversation, the focus and topic for the writing can be negotiated and refined. The purpose of this stage is to engage students in thinking about what they already know and beginning to develop new ideas from there.

**Articulate.** Invite students to decide precisely what they want written from the conversation that has taken place. Write this text down where the student can watch the progress and the process of the writing. It may be appropriate to discuss the conventions and structures of writing at this stage. During this process it should be made clear to the student how the speech and the writing come together.

**Integrate.** Engage students in reading and writing the text while it is being constructed. This will additionally highlight the interrelationship between reading, writing, speaking, and listening. Support the students in reading back the text when it is written. This will help the student to understand the nature of the integrated relationship between language modes.

**Demonstrate.** During this final stage, provide students with the opportunities to demonstrate their understanding of the links between spoken and written language by re-reading what they have written for themselves or what their teacher has written for them. Check that this written draft agrees with what they decided to write down from the initial conversation. By doing this, the teacher demonstrates for the student how the parts come together to form written text.

All teaching approaches can be analyzed in this way. It is helpful to do this for yourself in order to assess the strengths and weaknesses in your own classroom talk. Many of us are good at introducing a new activity, while others assume that students know exactly what is expected of them. Some teachers take an active part in the articulation stage but fail to put the pieces of the process back together again for the students and show them how to do it for themselves. Some students get confused quickly and fail to make progress with their schoolwork, while others fail to see the significance of their teacher's approach. Using a systematic framework to help shape classroom talk can aid in ensuring that students and teachers are constantly and successfully tuning in to each other, so that both benefit from the value of shared understandings.

### Audience

In taking the role of audience, teachers can act as a critical friend for students. They can contribute helpful advice and give appropriate feedback concerning the meanings that students are trying to shape. Acting as an audience, teachers can ask students to put their ideas differently to achieve clarification, they can help students extend their vocabulary, and they can reflect on their experiences as a listener themselves. Teachers can help students judge whether they have achieved what they set out to achieve. In these ways teachers can help students to begin to gain more control over their own learning.

Audiences need not only be teachers. They can be provided by others, including other students in the class, other members of the school, the community, and beyond. The more remote the audience from the students' shared experiences, the greater the demands on their language, the more they need to take account of assumptions that may not be shared, and the more they need to use language to be precise and accurate in terms of the meanings they wish to share.

## Conclusions

We teach speaking and listening for learning by engaging students in speaking and listening, by supporting and encouraging them, and by using speaking and listening in sharply focused ways. This style of talk may well be in contrast to that used in children's homes. Because of this children will need to learn the discourse of schooling. As teachers, our own speaking and listening behaviors have a powerful influence on students, acting as a model for them as we introduce new activities, as we talk with them about their work, as we discuss how we want them to proceed with activities, and as we explain how we generate criteria for judging success. In the same way, children's experiences of language use at home will influence the language repertoire they bring with them to school. Teachers have a clear responsibility to bridge this gap and to build on the language repertoire that all students bring with them into the classroom.

## References

Bruner, J.S. (1983). *Child's talk: Learning to use language.* New York: Norton.

Cazden, C.B. (1988). *The language of teaching and learning.* Portsmouth, NH: Heinemann.

Clay, M.M. (1998). *By different paths to common outcomes.* York, ME: Stenhouse.

Cloonan, A., Scull, J., & Turpin, H. (1998). *Teaching writers in the classroom.* Early Years Literacy Program, Stage 2. Melbourne, Australia: Longman.

Donaldson, M. (1978). *Children's minds.* Glasgow: Fontana Press.

Essex, G., & Raban, B. (2000). *Teaching speakers and listeners in the classroom.* Victoria, Australia: Addison Wesley Longman.

Fountas, I.C., & Pinnell, G.S. (1996). *Guided reading: Good first teaching for all children.* Portsmouth: NH: Heinemann.

Geekie, P., Cambourne, B., & Fitzsimmons, P. (1999). *Understanding literacy: Talking 'til you know what you mean.* Stoke-on-Trent, UK: Trentham Books.

Geekie, P., & Raban, B. (1993). *Learning to read and write through classroom talk.* Stoke-on-Trent, UK: Trentham Books.

Hannon, P. (1995). *Literacy at home and at school: Research and practice in teaching literacy with parents.* London: Falmer Press.

Heath, S.B. (1983). *Ways with words.* Cambridge, UK: Cambridge University Press.

Holdaway, D. (1979). *The foundations of literacy.* Auckland: Ashton Scholastic.

Howe, A. (1989). *Expanding horizons.* Sheffield, UK: National Association for Teachers of English.

Hughes, M., & Westgate, D. (1998). Possible enabling strategies in teacher-led talk with young pupils. *Language and Education, 12*(3), 174–191.

Jones, P. (Ed.). (1996). *Talking to learn.* Newtown, New South Wales, Australia: Primary English Teachers Association.

Norman, K. (Ed.). (1992). *Thinking voices.* London: Hodder & Stoughton.

Pigdon, K., & Woolley, M. (Eds.). (1992). *The big picture: Integrating children's learning.* Armidale, Victoria, Australia: Eleanor Curtin Publishing.

Reid, J., Forrestal, P., & Cook, J. (1989). *Small-group learning in the classroom.* PETA, New South Wales, Australia: Chalkface Press.

Snow, C.E. (1991). The theoretical basis for relationships between language and literacy development. *Journal of Research in Childhood Education, 6,* 30–46.

Vygotsky, L.S. (1962). *Thought and language.* Cambridge, MA: MIT Press.

Vygotsky, L.S. (1978). *Mind in society: The development of higher psychological processes.* (M. Cole, V.J. Steiner, S. Scribner, & E. Souberman, Eds. & Trans.). Boston: Harvard University Press. (Original work published 1934)

Wells, G. (1980). *Apprenticeship in meaning.* In K. Nelson (Ed.), *Children's language, Vol. 2* (pp. 81–96). New York: Gardiner.

Wells, G. (1986). *The meaning makers.* Portsmouth, NH: Heinemann.

Wood, D. (1998). *How children think and learn* (2nd ed.). Oxford, UK: Blackwell.

Wood, D., Bruner, J.S., & Ross, G. (1976). The role of tutoring in problem-solving. *Journal of Child Psychology and Psychiatry, 17,* 89–100.

# What's in *YOUR* Backpack? Exchanging Funds of Language Knowledge in an ESL Classroom

*Stacey King Medd and Kathryn F. Whitmore*

A small girl with jet-black hair enters the door of her new classroom. Her wire-rim glasses barely cover the panic in her eyes. Where are the familiar images of her old school—uniformed students, tidy lines of desks, and her teacher, "sun-sang-nym" at the front of the room? What do the dots, lines, and squiggles mean that are scattered on the brightly covered walls of this new place? She is just as mystified as she searches for meaning in the new patterns, inflections, and vocabulary she hears around her. Simplistic requests such as, "What do you want for lunch?" and "Will you be riding the bus?" compound her growing confusion. Once she has found a seat, she scans the room of children who seem to know exactly what to do and, with relief, spots a puzzle she can solve. The other boys and girls are emptying their backpacks. She can follow along because this task only involves unpacking what she has already brought to the classroom—a pencil box, a new notebook, and a lunch packed by her mother earlier in the day.

J i-Eun, like so many other children in today's classrooms, faces a myriad of challenges as she confronts her role as a second language learner. The most prominent challenge is to learn the content of the curriculum while acquiring a new language. Ji-Eun's English as a Second Language (ESL) teacher is similarly challenged—to help her become conversant in English in order to succeed academically and socially in her new school. How can teachers help children like Ji-Eun, a new student to the United States from Korea, unpack their intellectual and linguistic capabilities as well as their pencils? What curricular decisions will capitalize on Ji-Eun's existing knowledge (the linguistic, cognitive, and cultural material in her "backpack,") in order to support her future language learning?

In this chapter we present an illustration of what transpired when ESL students at Horace Mann Elementary School in Iowa City, Iowa, USA were invited by their teacher, Stacey Medd (the first author of this chapter), to explore their own identities and those of their classmates through a theme study that celebrated family stories. Kathy Whitmore (the second author) was a colearner and observer during many of the events described. The children you will meet in the vignettes that follow came from a wide range of academic, linguistic, and socioeconomic backgrounds from all over the world. Some of their families were living temporarily in the United States while the parents completed graduate school. Others had sought new employment opportunities in the United States or were political refugees. Regardless, the children shared a common characteristic: They wanted to know more about each other as they forged friendships in a new environment. The classroom descriptions in this chapter illustrate a sociocultural theory of language development. We selected these representative data excerpts to argue that inviting second language students to use their first and second languages and cultures to teach each other supports learning to talk in an additional language—in this case, English. More specifically, the following four tenets of sociocultural theory were put into practice to help young language learners reach their intellectual and academic potentials, even in a new language system:

- activation of both individual and collective zones of proximal development (Moll & Whitmore, 1993; Vygotsky, 1978)

- initial focus on sign systems other than oral and written language (Leland & Harste, 1994) followed by incorporation of the additional language

- regular talk about and response to high-quality children's literature (Daniels, 1994; Short & Pierce, 1990)

- sharing and exchanging children's existing funds of knowledge (Moll, Amanti, Neff, & Gonzalez, 1992; Moll & Whitmore, 1993).

As the children discovered new concepts about the people and places represented in their classroom community, they grew as communicators and knowledge seekers. Plus, the authentic reasons and audiences for talking in a second language made learning flourish.

## Unpacking Our Art Supplies, Adding a New Language

In a children's picture book by Aliki (1998) titled *Marianthe's Story: Painted Words, Spoken Memories*, a knowledgeable teacher demonstrates the potential for using art as a communication tool. He asks Marianthe, a frightened new ESL student, to share her ideas and feelings via her beautiful artistic creations. Later, when language is attached to the visual depictions and Marianthe's story is shared for a second time, her expertise with her life story allows her to take the position of the classroom teacher. As a result, the lessons she shares with her peers have a transformative affect on her classroom community.

Fortunately, when teachers find ways to layer oral and written language over experiences that emphasize other sign systems, this scenario does not have to be limited to the pages of Aliki's book. Short and Harste (1996) explain,

> Sign sytems are alternative ways of creating and sharing meaning with others such as language, mathematics, music, art, and movement. In schools, language has been overemphasized as *the* way of constructing meaning, and the other systems are treated as frills and talents of only a few…. When we are unable to use a particular system, there are meanings we can never know or communicate to others. (p. 259)

Many experiences in the family stories theme study took advantage of Stacey's students' facility with multiple-sign systems to communicate with their peers. Eventually, developmental forms of the target language (English) accompanied a variety of products, as you will see in the three representative activities explained in this section—collaboratively constructing the learning enviroment, creating storyboard drawings, and producing personal scrapbooks.

### Learning Environments

"Risk," says Fletcher (1993), "allows children to outgrow themselves" (p. 17). Providing second language learners with a comfortable, inviting learning environment is essential if children are going to feel safe enough to risk experimenting with a second language. A safe environment in which children see themselves visually represented and feel a sense of ownership lowers children's affective filters so that risk taking is more likely and new language is more comprehensible (Krashen, 1985).

To prepare Stacey's ESL room for learning about family stories and to facilitate the students' ownership of the classroom space, the children constructed family trees from cardboard carpet tubes. Each child added a branch with leaves attached to represent their significant family members. Some leaves, like Wei's (see Figure 1), included dual language representations, and many conversations evolved as the learners observed their peers' collections. The students counted Wei's English and Chinese additions to the tree, and articulated concepts such as, "He has more than Gao, but Sakura has the most!" Such comparative language enabled the children to experiment with ways of communicating discoveries about numerical information related to their families. The experience also let the children know very directly that they can use their native language in the ESL classroom.

Soon the children added large self-portraits to the room to accompany the family trees, and "memory bubbles" that contained sketches of important family moments emerged. These drawings were springboards for sharing stories

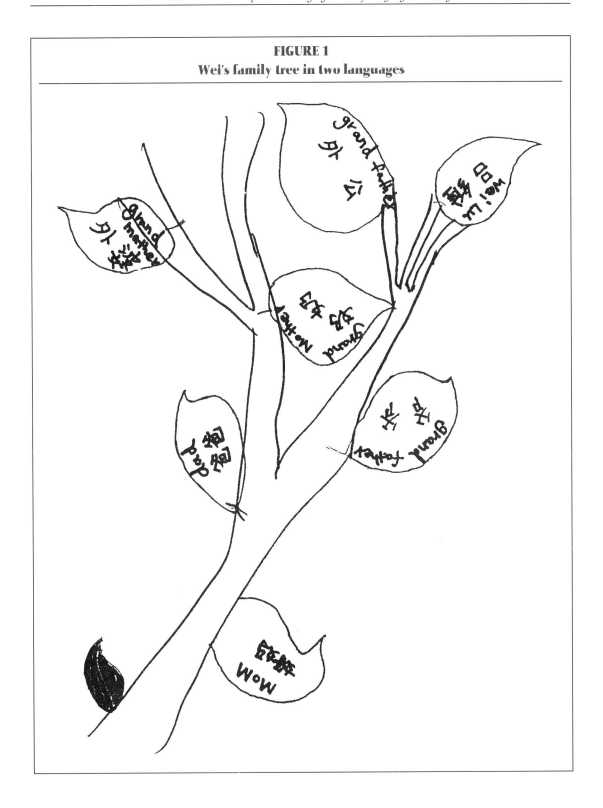

**FIGURE 1**
**Wei's family tree in two languages**

through a variety of linguistic means. Roberto, a first-grade student from Colombia, found a story worth telling as he added the final touches on his depiction of a fishing scene in his memory bubble (see our reproduction in Figure 2). Stacey had not previously been aware of Roberto's fishing expertise, and she asked him to tell her more about his memory. Soon other students became involved in his sharing. Their questions evolved from simple structures and familiar content—"Do you like fish?"—to more complex structures and specific content—"What bait you use walleye?"—as language was used to exchange increasingly sophisticated knowledge. Roberto stretched his language abilities and confidence as his excitement coaxed short phrases from one-word utterances. What a delight when fishing magazines eventually traveled from Roberto's home to the classroom via his sturdy backpack.

Visual prompts such as those described are critical in second language development. It is difficult to juggle multiple demanding tasks at one time. As children recreate a family story, for example, they piece together relevant sequential and descriptive information. Partnering those demands with a need to communicate in a second language may make the request overwhelming. Inviting children to accomplish the primary re-creation using another sign system such as art helped to make the linguistic challenge attainable.

## Storyboard Drawings

In another example, creating storyboard drawings before audiotaping retellings of favorite family stories offered ESL students an invitation to sequence their stories and add details in an activity that was initially language-free. The children sketched the highlights of important events in a family story on adhesive notes. After arranging the notes sequentially, they thought of sound effects to accompany their pictures and made them using a wide array of tools ranging from musical instuments to kitchen utensils. Layering sound onto drawing added meaning to the stories and made their creation more fun. Only then, after manipulating two manageable sign systems (drawing and sounds), did the second language learners engage in the more challenging task of retelling the stories in English. Following lots of practice, with children supporting each other's attempts and generating multiple revisions, the stories were audiotaped. Transcripts of the tapes were later examined for evidence of emerging strengths. Consequently, the end products were not only delightful, they provided authentic documentation of the children's development (i.e. approximations being used, strategies employed, self-corrections) and vital information about family backgrounds. Figure 3 shows Ji-Eun's drawn storyboard and written family story labeled with sound effects.

## Personal Scrapbooks

Over the many weeks of the family stories theme study, children's construction of personal scrapbooks facilitated similar language learning success

**FIGURE 2**
**Memory bubble**

## FIGURE 3
### Storyboard and text for Ji-Eun's family story

My name is Ji-Eun, and this is my family story. When I was sleeping (deep breaths into microphone) my mom and my dad went to the hospital. (can opener) They, when they got to the hospital, they were walking very fast. (maracas) The next day me and my grandma and my dad went to the hospital, and my mom was sleeping. (deep breathing ) And I wake my mom up. I aks, I ask, "What time my mom, my baby gonna come?" My mom said, "Just a few while. " And I waited and waited and waited. (spoon on pan like a clock tolling)

And my baby camed, and it was a girl. She was sleeping. (deep breaths in and out) And then my father said, "Let's take this baby to home," and we taked it.

And one night I sleep, sleep, I was sleeping, and (deep breaths) and my baby cried (cry) and I wake up. I sing my lullaby, (Korean lullaby) by layering talk onto art work and artifacts. All students have interesting lives that they bring to the classroom, and samples of those lives can be brought to the pages of scrapbooks to form valuable language introductions. Photographs prompt opportunities for questioning as children's curiosity tends to over-power their inhibition to learn more about each other or to use English. When sharing takes place prior to scrapbook writing, young authors also gain insight into their audience.

To get their scrapbooks started, Stacey's students gathered scrapbook material from family adventures both inside and outside the home. A ticket stub suggested detailed descriptions of a movie's plot. An invitation to a party paved the way for comparing and contrasting birthday traditions. Postcards gathered on family road trips introduced the group to powerful geographic terminology. Even packaging from a product was useful, as students shared directions used in preparing food or assembling a toy.

As students glued their personal mementos to scrapbook pages, they also attached meaning to the spoken English used. Each question and comment from the children offered Stacey evaluative information regarding shifts in language construction, vocabulary acquisition, and risk taking. The basic principles remained the same—students were empowered to travel further linguistically when they were fueled by the familiar. Written English was more accessible when it accompanied a real-world experience and tangible nonlinguistic artifacts.

Curricular engagements like family trees, storyboards, and scrapbooks opened pathways for the children to express their previous knowledge, construct new knowledge, and communicate regardless of their facility with English. The engagements instilled a sense of personal identity, invited multiple inter-pretations, and inspired the children's confidence to ask real questions. Because the organizational focus of the activities described in this section was at the in-dividual level, however, Stacey wanted to add more social learning experiences that would nudge children toward negotiating a shared meaning. After all, "Language did not develop because there was one language user, but two, and they wished to communicate" (Short & Harste, 1996, p. 55).

## Exchanging the Stuff in Our Backpacks

Literature study groups are a powerful way to organize second language readers in order to explore cultural identities and relevant social and political is-sues while enjoying quality literature—particularly picture books (Freeman & Freeman, 1994; Whitmore & Crowell, 1994). The family stories theme study took advantage of the abundance of rich illustrations and written texts available in the intersection between "family" and "multicultural" bodies of children's litera-ture. Because Stacey's focus was on constructing a shared meaning for texts that her students probably could not read independently, she often read the books aloud or had children participate in paired reading. We offer three examples to illustrate how student-initiated questions opened all kinds of possibilities for collaborative response that activated both individual and collective zones of proximal development in the children's talking and learning (Moll & Whitmore, 1993; Vygotsky, 1978). These examples are particularly interesting because at this point the children had developed a strong background in using multiple sign systems to strengthen their oral language communication in English.

## Collaborating Through Talk

One group of four first and second graders from Korea and China listened to *Nana Upstairs, Nana Downstairs* by Tomie dePaola (1973)—a moving book exploring a young boy's memories of his grandmother and great-grandmother. In response, the students made a list of important ideas represented in the story and decided how to represent each idea visually on a collage of images and materials. The task challenged the developing collaborative skills of this particular mixture of strong personalities, so the language they used included problem solving as well as reader response content. For example, students questioned each other about the importance of their chosen story elements. Ting forced Chen-Chen to defend the importance of adding a depiction of Nana's hair to the collage, and Chen-Chen defended her position by returning to the text for confirmation. Because she shared a strong bond with her own grandmother, she also elaborated on her personal history. As more opinions were tossed into the exchange, Ji-Eun decided that an organizational tool was necessary. She grabbed a tablet and created two columns, one listing ideas for the collage and the other itemizing materials needed. The multidimensional collage they eventually created exemplified their shared understanding of the process and the text.

## Exchanging Knowledge Through Talk

Another discussion took place after two students read *Too Many Tamales* by Gary Soto (1993), a book that features a Latino family making tamales. Second-year ESL students Igor, a third grader from Russia, and José, a fourth grader from Mexico, engaged in paired reading of *Too Many Tamales*, following which Stacey participated in the discussion. In the following classroom discussion, José teaches Igor new vocabulary, and Igor differentiates between fiction and nonfiction for José. As you will see, the book prompted an intellectual exchange of cultural knowledge that included lessons on geography, cooking, and immigration even though the boys' English was at a developmental level.

The question that initiated the discussion was asked by José. It stemmed from the conflict he saw between the story's cultural content and its setting. He asked, "Why was it snowing? In what place was it?" Because José immediately associated the story event with his home in Mexico, the out-of-place snow perplexed him.

Igor offered the first hypothesis in reply. "Maybe in a part of Mexico," he said. This made sense because Igor's knowledge of Latin culture was limited to his friendship with José.

"There is just one place in Mexico that it snows," said José. "The house looks like United States. In Mexico it would snow, but degrees get hotter. Not stay like that in the picture. Only flurries."

"What is flurries?" asked Igor.

"Tiny snow. Small snow."

"Oh. Maybe a house in Texas."

"Texas doesn't snow a lot," said José. "It just snows in mountain. I think the author didn't think about that. That book is not about science. Like the author didn't think that. It's not real."

Igor agreed and labeled the concept José was explaining, "It's just a fiction book."

At this point, Stacey asked, "Do most of the things seem real in the book?"

"The author just wanted to write the story his family. He wanted thing to made the picture prettier. He want snow. I don't know if Argentina there's tamales. Is there?" asked José.

Igor said, "I think we can figure it out." He turned to the front of the book. "It says New York. In here," he said as he pointed to the words on the copyright page.

José said, "Made in New York. Not story in New York!"

Igor pointed to another illustration. "The picture says *manteca* [butter]. Is that in Spain?"

"It's not city," José explained, "It's like my grandma used it. Probably something like flour. Not a city. An ingredient."

After a pause, José continued hypothesis building. "Probably a Mexican family in the United States. In West Liberty [Iowa], there is many people from Mexico there. They have stores with stuff like that. It's in like a city that people from Mexico come there and make their stores. I went just once there. My mom pick me up from school. We went to eat the Mexican restaurant. I want a toy there. We went to buy some bread. My mom said, 'Not a toy. Candy.'"

Stacey asked, "Igor, do you think that is possible?"

"It might not be West Liberty. Another place like that," he answered.

"Yeah, Omaha. New York. Some Mexican people there. New Mexico snows sometimes. Rocky Mountains make snow."

"Yeah, one of the states in America," Igor agreed.

"Igor, do you make Russian foods at your house?" asked Stacey.

"Yeah, Russian and American."

"When you look out your window, does it look like Russia?"

"No, in Russia there is not a lot of fields. Just woods."

"When you come to a new place, what happens?" Stacey asked.

Igor answered again, "You miss food from your country. Sometimes my mom make it. But sometimes we have Japanese noodles instead. Very easy."

"Yeah," concluded José, "In United States many food. In the south, biscuits. South Carolina, hamburgers. Pasta."

José, Igor, and Stacey's conversation illustrates the depth of talk that can occur when even novice language learners are intent on resolving issues and answering questions about engaging texts. Each participant was a mediator in each other's individual zone of proximal development, nudging each other toward new concepts about the world by sharing their own knowledge. In fact, none of the participants (even Stacey) attended to the developmental form of English that José and Igor used. Their focus was on the function of talk to exchange funds of knowledge in order to strengthen their response to the text.

## Building Collective Knowledge Through Talk

A similar conversation took place among a different group of first-year ESL students discussing the book *Dumpling Soup* by Jama Kim Rattigan (1993) after Stacey read it aloud. This story involves a family preparing for New Year festivities, but there is a mixture of Korean, Chinese, and Japanese cultures portrayed in the illustrations. The group of ESL readers represented the same cultural mix—Jung-Hu and Un-Jung were sixth graders from Korea, Gao and Wei were third graders from China, and Satomi was a fifth grader from Japan. These children's English proficiency was just emerging, and yet just like José and Igor, they maintained a complex discussion focused first on determining the geography of the story's setting.

> Satomi asked, "Where are they? It is New Year, but shorts and shirts like this."
>
> Wei responded, "Colombia. It's down. It's hot."
>
> Satomi differentiated between the physical characteristics of the Asian children in the book and Latino children in Colombia by showing illustrations in the text and said, "But face and skin not."
>
> Wei shared another idea stating, "Brazil."
>
> Jung-Hu had been a silent observer up to this point. Suddenly and adamantly he flipped through the pages of the book and pointed out geographical attributes. "Noodles not! Is Hawaii. Trees many!" he exclaimed.
>
> At this point Gao's eyes lit up as he zipped to the shelf to retrieve the globe, a powerful tool for relaying his message. His excited fingers traveled the circumference of the globe as he said, "All around the equator. Because is very hot. All time hot. Never winter. Congo. This one!"
>
> Meanwhile, Satomi had been rereading the beginning of the text while listening to Gao and had made a discovery. "Is Oahu. Look," she stated as she read aloud a portion of the words. "Where is Oahu?" she asked Stacey, who answered by posing another question. "How can we find out?"
>
> Gao and Wei examined the globe while Satomi and Jung-Hu headed for the atlas and even remembered to use the index.
>
> Later, Jung-Hu, feeling good about his initial conclusion, responded with a confident, "Yeah, is Hawaii!"

Although students in this third group used many more approximations of conventional English and were more limited in terms of language structures and vocabulary, the discussion still included rich cognitive and social challenges. Students were able to share many inquiry strategies they had acquired related to finding information and they used their collective cultural backgrounds as a foundation for asking questions. Later, their fascinating discussion of family New Year traditions continued and was displayed visually through the use of a Venn diagram (see Figure 4). Un-Jung, a newcomer who had remained silent during the intense earlier discussion, chose to join in at this point. Her contribution—adding the word *han-bok* (traditional dress) in Korean to the diagram—signaled her first participation in the coconstruction of shared knowledge of the class.

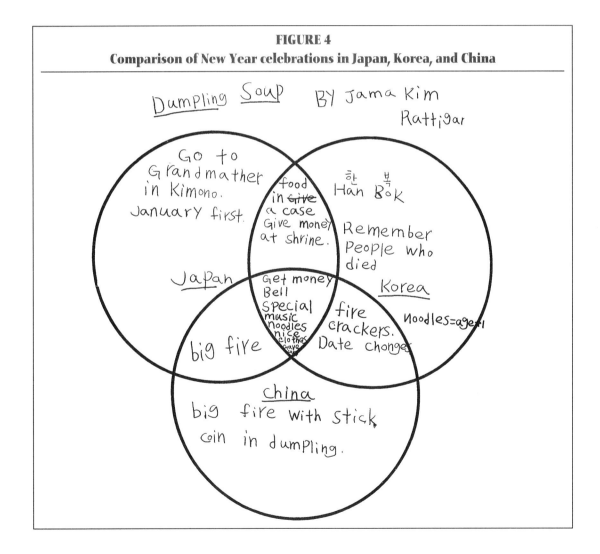

**FIGURE 4**

**Comparison of New Year celebrations in Japan, Korea, and China**

# Goodbye/Hello

These students unpacked their linguistic, intellectual, and cultural capabilities along with their pencils and lunches from their backpacks while investigating family stories in their ESL classroom. To them, language was much more than a set of grammatical rules that only apply to English. As she sat side by side with these learners, listening to their offerings and inquiries, it was critical that Stacey consider guiding questions like those proposed by Taylor (1993) to assess their language development.

What's happening?

What's going on?

How do these children create order out of the complexities of their everyday lives?

How does this child construct and use language?

How does this child become a member of a community of learners?

How does this child theorize about doing? (p. 58)

For the children, language became a set of linguistic processes that are exercised across the globe: informing, questioning, constructing, creating, and confirming. For Stacey, each reflective response offered the power to move assessment closer to authenticity and teacher closer to child.

This ESL classroom is an active sociocultural system where children act as mediators for each other in individual and collective zones of proximal development. Through activities like those described here, the children interdependently exchange social and cultural resources to learn a new language.

Later in the school year, the young girl with jet-black hair and glasses bounds excitedly into a classroom that accepts the form of her English and envelopes her family history. This setting is no longer foreign to Ji-Eun. Her life-sized self-portrait smiles down from the wall. Strains of her own voice singing a familiar Korean lullaby can be accessed at the touch of a tape player's button, and a scrapbook on the shelf holds personal mementos of her past. Ji-Eun and her classmates have brought their world to the classroom to exchange with others, and she is now more empowered to make sense of new sets of words, faces, and expectations.

The poem that follows, thoughtfully composed by Ji-Eun during the family stories study, beautifully expresses the reality that her past and future are no longer so distant from each other.

Goodbye, my teacher, that helped me.
Goodbye, Grandma, always gave me money for cookies.
Goodbye, my best friend, that play sand tag with me.

Goodbye, Korea!
Hello, My Mr. Gardner and Mrs. Medd.
Hello, Dad that stayed here until I came.
Hello, My new friend Lucie that helped me to learn English.
Hello, America!!!

# References

Daniels, H. (1994). *Literature circles: Voice and choice in the student-centered classroom.* York, ME: Stenhouse.

Fletcher, R. (1993). *What a writer needs.* Portsmouth, NH: Heinemann.

Freeman, D.E., & Freeman, Y.S. (1994). *Between worlds: Access to second language acquisition.* Portsmouth, NH: Heinemann.

Krashen, S. (1985). *Inquiries and insights.* Haywood, CA: Alemany Press.

Leland, C., & Harste, J. (1994). Multiple ways of knowing: Curriculum in a new key. *Language Arts, 71*(5), 337–345.

Moll, L.C., Amanti, C., Neff, D., & Gonzalez, N. (1992). Funds of knowledge for teaching: Using a qualitative approach to connect homes and classrooms. *Theory into practice, XXXI*(2), 132–141.

Moll, L.C., & Whitmore, K.F. (1993). Vygotsky in classroom practice: Moving from individual transmission to social transaction. In E.A. Foreman, N. Minick, & C.A. Stone (Eds.), *Contexts for learning: Sociocultural dynamics in children's development.* New York: Oxford University Press.

Short, K., & Harste, J.C. (with Burke, C.) (1996). *Creating classrooms for authors and inquiries.* Portsmouth, NH: Heinemann.

Short, K.G., & Pierce, K.M. (1990). *Talking about books: Creating literate communities.* Portsmouth, NH: Heinemann.

Taylor, D. (1993). *From the child's point of view.* Portsmouth, NH: Heinemann.

Vygotsky, L.S. (1978). *Mind in society: The development of higher psychological processes.* (M. Cole, V.J. Steiner, S. Scribner, & E. Souberman, Eds. & Trans.). Boston: Harvard University Press. (Original work published 1934)

Whitmore, K.F., & Crowell, C.G. (1994). *Inventing a classroom.* York, ME: Stenhouse.

# For Further Reading

Freeman, Y.S., & Freeman, D.E. (1998). *ESL/EFL teaching: Principles for success.* Portsmouth, NH: Heinemann.

Fu, D. (1995). *"My trouble is my English": Asian students and the American dream.* Portsmouth, NH: Heinemann.

Winston, L. (1997). *Keepsakes: Using family stories in elementary classrooms.* Portsmouth, NH: Heinemann.

Zemelman, S., Bearden, P., Simmons, Y., & Leki, P. (2000). *History comes home: Family stories across the curriculum.* York, ME: Stenhouse.

# Children's Books Cited

Aliki. (1998). *Marianthe's story: Painted words, spoken memories.* New York: Greenwillow.

dePaola, T. (1973). *Nana upstairs, Nana downstairs.* New York: Putnam.

Rattigan, J.K. (1993). *Dumpling soup.* Boston: Little, Brown.

Soto, G. (1993). *Too many tamales.* Ill. E. Martinez. New York: Putnam.

### More Children's Literature

Jin, S. (1996). *My first American friend.* Boston: Houghton Mifflin.
Johnson, A. (1989). *Tell me a story, Mama.* New York: Orchard Books.
Parker, R.A. (1990). *Grandfather Tang's story.* New York: Crown.
Wing, N. (1996). *Jalapeno bagels.* New York: Atheneum.

# Practical Suggestions for Supporting Speaking and Listening in Classrooms

*Dale Gordon*

**W**hat talk do we hear, and what do we see when we listen to and watch children at work in classrooms? Who is talking and who is listening? Do we see children with heads together chatting as they work, sharing important personal news and retelling stories; organizing their play and planning activities; talking about their families and inviting friends to come over; discussing their schoolwork and asking each other questions? They may be asking, What do I write here, How did you do that, Do you have the same answer as I do, How do you spell that, and What does that mean? Is there a quiet hum of relaxed and contented talk? Are there periods of quiet, not because children are asked to work in silence but because there are natural breaks in talk as children finish what they are saying and attend to their work?

We should see and hear all these things because this is informal talk—the normal, everyday social interaction of all groups of people when they are together and when they are comfortable with each other's company. Students share their viewpoints, their ideas, their plans, and their hopes; they also share companionable silences, all the while learning from each other.

*Engaging in social talk is fundamental to our society, and we need to give children time and opportunity in classrooms to practice emerging speaking and listening skills as they develop and learn to use effective and satisfying interpersonal communication with others.*

As well, there are conventions that our society uses to provide a framework for engaging in more structured speaking and listening interactions. Each oral language text has discrete conventions that apply to it and that are used for particular purposes and audiences. These conventions determine the ways we present ideas, opinions, and information. A formal debate before an audience and a judge has different rules for speaking and listening than an argument between two classmates. A newsreader reporting on a baseball game will present it in formal ways quite different from a casual explanation of "how we won the game" told to friends. Understanding how the range of oral language texts work is also part of learning about talk, and using them appropriately gives us ways to communicate our meanings more fully with others.

*We need to establish classroom structures and procedures for children to develop under-standings of the forms oral language texts take and provide opportunities within purposeful contexts for children to "have a go" at using them.*

Cultivating a classroom culture where speaking and listening are learned and practiced requires more than just allowing talk to happen. It takes planning to provide authentic opportunities for using formal oral texts, to develop a classroom environment where children can feel relaxed and comfortable in experimenting with talk and where talk does not become a management problem in terms of noise, off-task behavior, and distress to others.

How should we manage talk in our classrooms? Luckily, there are many ways of strategically planning to help children become good oral language users. Also, there are many ways of assessing children's oral language. The wise teacher will make sure that assessment procedures are integral to learning and that they provide explicit data about children's speaking and listening development to guide and direct lesson planning.

## Modeling the Conventions of Social Discourse

As the most experienced and adept speaker and listener in the classroom, it is up to the teacher to model the look and sound of social talk, and to demonstrate the behaviors it anticipates—taking turns, listening, planning, expressing ideas and information, and responding to others. Good teachers value time spent talking with children and respond to children's conversation in the same way that they respond to other adults—with courtesy, care, and attention. Observing children's behaviors as they talk with each other will allow the teacher to determine how well children understand the conventions of social discourse. Making sure that not all the classroom talk is directed by the teacher or through the teacher is crucial to children's speaking and listening development.

### Providing Opportunities for Children to Practice Social Discourse

Children need to experiment with speaking and listening in the same way as they draft their writing or practice reading. It takes practice to build competent and confident talk. Teachers can value learning to talk and learning to listen by scheduling specific times for these activities and planning the daily program so there is plenty of opportunity for children to engage in talk. Planned discussion times during which children share personal experiences and knowledge or discuss an issue or topic are good opportunities for children to learn how social talk works, and to practice it for their own particular purposes and within defined boundaries where it is OK to "have a go." Teachers can schedule time and organize the classroom for any of the following activities.

*Morning talk*—when children can share personal news in social groups. Vary the size and composition of the groups from time to time to give children the opportunity to experience talk with different people.

*News reporting sessions*—allow time for children to report and discuss local school and community news as well as national and international news.

*"Share and compare" conference groups*—have children talk about their work with each other. This is valuable talking and listening where children can test their own understandings of the work against those of their peers, taking into account the views of others as they explore a given topic.

*Brainstorming and concept mapping sessions*—involve children in discussion of a topic in which they can verbalize the links and connections they make with the topic, as well as allowing for the exploration of others' knowledge and experiences of it.

Vary the ways in which children are grouped for work sessions. There are many ways of grouping, and each one has advantages for talking and listening. Some types of groupings that can be used are as follows:

*Heterogeneous groups*

1. mixed sex and single sex groups

2. friendship groups

3. cross-age groups

*Homogeneous groups*

1. interest groups

2. skill-learning groups

3. specific needs groups

*Cooperative groups*

1. jigsaw groups (Divide the class into groups. Each group investigates just one aspect of a topic, and at the conclusion of the time they share their information to provide the "whole story" of the topic—fitting it together like a jigsaw)

2. 1, 2, 3 groups (Group 1—individuals plan what they think and will say, Group 2—individuals take a partner to "pair and share," Group 3—three pairs meet as a larger group to reach a consensus view to present to the whole group)

3. Expert groups

Teachers also can make opportunities to engage children in informal talk at times by greeting them when they come into class, chatting with them while they work or while they eat lunch, and starting conversations in the schoolyard or outside in the community. These authentic conversations engage children and the teacher in talking and listening to each other for real purposes. Learning to talk for real purposes is also facilitated by giving children classroom responsibilities in which talk is part of the task. Teachers can have children invite others in the school community to visit and share an activity, greet and introduce classroom visitors, and explain classroom activities to them. Students should be encourged to take verbal messages to others (rather than notes written by the teacher); discuss ways to organize and delegate group responsibilities; plan and inform others of the day's schedule; and take responsibility for maintaining lists, checking tasks, and collecting information.

# Establishing Guidelines for Social Discourse

Help children understand that it is acceptable to engage in talk while they work. Discuss their rights and responsibilities for this social talk; for example, they have a right to talk to each other and they have a right to complete school tasks in an environment where they can work effectively, but others do, too. In order for everyone to be comfortable, the noise level of social talk must not interfere with others' rights.

Establish the boundaries and highlight expected behaviors, procedures, and processes. With the children, develop reference wall charts that list what good speakers and listeners do, and have children refer to these so their behaviors match expectations. Use the reference charts in Figure 1 to develop assessment checklists that will let you see at a glance how individual children are engaging in social discourse.

### Teaching Listening Skills

Effective listening skills can be taught through a variety of methods. Playing listening games such as "pass the whisper" (also called "telephone") and telling progressive stories can teach children the importance of good listening in a fun atmosphere. Teachers should encourage and reward good listening with specific praise that highlights the effective listening behaviors they have observed the children using.

Children also enjoy serial reading and reading and listening to taped stories. List available story tapes on a chart and have a "booking" system for children to preplan independent listening. Read and retell strategies are useful for ascertaining the effectiveness of the students' listening.

Teachers can promote enthusiasm for listening activities by collecting a wide range of listening and speaking materials for classroom experiences. A

---

**FIGURE 1**
**Good listener, good speaker wall chart**

| A GOOD LISTENER | A GOOD SPEAKER |
|---|---|
| • faces the speaker | • faces the listener(s) |
| • responds with his or her whole body, keeping it still to listen, nodding and shaking head in response to the speaker | • knows what he or she want to say and thinks about it, thinks about the listener and plans to match what he or she says with this listener |
| • waits for the right pause to reply | • varies voice to say it better |
| • paraphrases the speaker's ideas and information to affirm meaning | • checks that the listener understands before going further |
| • asks focused questions | • asks focused questions |
| • uses gestures to support and add further information | • uses gestures to support and add further information |
| • maintains eye contact | • maintains eye contact |
| • pauses for speaker to respond | • pauses for the listener to respond |
| • gives opportunities for speaker to respond | • gives opportunities for the listener to respond |

---

read–along and listening center, complete with audiotapes, tape players, a compact disc player, microphones, and other oral presentation devices can make a good resource collection.

## Planning Classroom Seating Arrangements to Facilitate Classroom Discourse

Classroom seating arrangements have a direct impact on the quantity and quality of talk in the classroom. Talk will not happen if desks are in rows or facing the same direction. If it does, it will be constrained and possibly disruptive as children raise their voices to be heard while seeking to overcome the physical difficulties of talking to each other. Children's seating and desks should be arranged in groups of varying sizes, with children sitting facing each other to support and encourage talk. A class meeting place where the whole class and smaller groups can gather could be set up, either adjacent to the class library shelves or children's work displays, or where there is good access to audiovisual equipment.

# Promoting Emotional Expression and Conflict Resolution Through Role Plays

Children need to be given opportunities to practice expressing their emotions and feelings and supporting the expressed emotional needs of others by listening and responding to them. Children need to know how to discuss issues and put them in perspective, to direct the responses needed for their own and others' well being, and to listen and respond to others in ways that will allow for win-win conclusions to conversations.

Role plays provide opportunities for children to experience different and difficult roles and to put themselves in others' shoes. Students can take on the roles of a parent, a member of a minority group, another classmate who has a different viewpoint, or a leader choosing a team. Activities such as these give children practice in what to do in difficult real-life situations by setting up scenarios for discussion such as what to do if you see someone doing the wrong thing, what to do if you feel you are being treated unfairly, how to make peace with your best friend after an argument, and how to speak as a team leader when the team loses.

Role plays also provide children with ways of speaking assertively (e.g., "Please do not do that to me; When you do _____ I feel _____, and I do not like it; Stop doing that now please") and they give them practice in taking roles in which they need to make and justify decisions. Through role plays, students can practice valuable skills such as setting up and following procedures for class meetings; taking turns at performing cooperative group roles like speaker, judge, observer, or reporter; and discussing issues from a number of angles.

Appointing an observer who will use the observation checklist in Figure 2 to record speaking and listening behaviors is a highly effective way of assessing students' participation in these activities. Reporting back to the whole group is a valuable part of the observer's role. It is at this time that children have the opportunity to reflect on their speaking and listening behavior and learn from their peers what is acceptable and what is not.

The teacher will be able to use this reporting session to inform his or her assessment of children's speaking and listening behaviors. Discussion questions such as those that follow will assist the group in developing their ability to articulate the parameters of group talking and listening.

- How can people show they are listening and accepting other's opinions and ideas?
- How can we ensure that everyone is able to have a turn—what words do we use to let them know it is OK to speak?
- How can we encourage shy people to join in?
- How can we encourage talkative people to let others have a turn?
- How do we reach agreement? How do we know when we have?
- How can we avoid wasting time?

---

**FIGURE 2**
**Listening to group talk: Observational record**

|  | always | never |
|---|---|---|
| people took turns to speak in our group | | |
| each person was encouraged to speak in our group | | |
| we said: | | |
| | | |
| people really listened to each other | | |
| everyone had a chance to contribute | | |
| we were able to reach an agreement | | |
| we decided to: | | |
| | | |
| the time was used well | | |

---

# Learning the Conventions of Oral Language Texts

If we want children to know the conventions of oral language texts, understand how they work, and bring these into their personal repertoires, we must give children opportunities to use a range of these texts in the classroom.

### Fictional Oral Texts

Storytelling can provide opportunities for imaginative talk because much of human experience and wisdom is passed on through story. Plan classroom experiences that give children the opportunity to use talk to create, to develop expression of fantasy, to use their imaginations, and to retell their own and others' stories. Children need to know how to tell a story, and a good place to start is by having them tell fictional stories. Story*telling* can lead to story*writing* and *reading*. Because it is difficult for most children to stand up and tell a story, they may need ideas and props to help them get started with storytelling. Try some of the following ideas for storytelling in the classroom.

*Memorable moments—Pick a photograph.* Collect a box of photographs, old postcards, greeting cards, or photographs from newspapers or magazines. Children can then choose a photo and make up a story about it.

*Memorable moments—Pick a card.* Make a set of cards with a "memorable moment" idea starter on each card like the examples in Figure 3. Have children choose a card and make up a story beginning with the story starter on the card.

*Something special—The storybox.* Collect interesting and unusual objects to go in the storybox—jewelry, pocketbooks, household items, toys, tools, and clothes are all good objects to include. Then have the students each choose a special object from the storybox, and start a story by saying, "This means a lot to me because...."

Alternatively, children could each bring their own "something special" into the classroom from home.

*"Luck of the draw" stories.* To prepare for this activity, teachers can use the suggestions in Figure 4 to make three sets of cards representing characters, settings, and conflicts, which will then be put into separate boxes. This is a good storytelling activity for small groups or partners. Children take one or two cards from each box and use them to plan a story that integrates the character or characters, the conflict, and the setting from the cards they have chosen. Further cards can be taken, but whatever is written on them must be used in the story.

*Dress up a story.* Collect a box or basket of "dress-ups"—hats, gloves, parts of costumes, clothes from other eras, evening wear, bags and pocketbooks, scarves and cloaks, spectacle frames, belts, sashes, and masks can all be included. Children can choose clothing from the box and create a story about the character they have become.

*Add a story.* Children or the teacher read a given story and then continue it by making up what happens next.

*Never-ending stories.* Sitting in a circle, the first group (or child) starts a story, and each group or child in turn adds the next episode. When the story returns to the first group they can choose to end it or they can conclude the session

---

**FIGURE 3**
**Storytelling starter ideas**

| | |
|---|---|
| The happiest moment of my life was… | It all started when… |
| I was terrified when… | I was *so* embarrassed… |
| You won't believe this but… | How was I to know that… |
| The worst day of my life began… | The funniest thing that ever happened to me… |
| Early this morning… | It was so unexpected I was … |

---

**FIGURE 4**
**"Luck of the draw" storytelling cards**

| CHARACTERS | SETTINGS | CONFLICTS |
|---|---|---|
| a lost baby | a musty attic | the bike tire was flat |
| two pirates | a deserted building | the beast continued to follow them |
| a lonely old man | a dark cave | they were being pushed into it |
| a cunning cat burglar | a peaceful country village | the door slammed shut |
| a cheating friend | a yacht in the Bahamas | they were surrounded |
| a clever detective | a circus ring | it was a perfect crime |
| an evil witch | a windowless tower | they were alone and very frightened |
| a spoiled child | at a football game | what would happen now? |
| an impatient cyclist | a busy shopping center | they were running short of food |
| a repentant thief | a damp cellar | the water was rising |
| a group of school children | deep in the forest | they lost sight of her |
| a mad professor | in the schoolyard | smoke was billowing from it |
| a persistent salesperson | a crowded airport | who had taken their bags? |
| a good fairy | in the laboratory | the bridge had collapsed |
| an angry police officer | in the days of the knights of the round table | the precious diamond was gone |

---

with a cliff-hanger that will need to be continued next session. The teacher can vary this game by changing the rules. Some variations include

- banning the use of particular words—e.g., *then, and, after;*
- mandating the use of words or key phrases for every episode—e.g., *yellow, wicked, ice-cream,* "and then the baby began to cry," or "'I don't care!' shouted the bear";
- deciding that each episode must have the first word beginning with the next letter of the alphabet (episode one: *A*nastasia always hated going to her great aunt's house because her aunt…; episode two: *B*ut this time was going to be different…; episode three: *C*limbing into the carriage she…); and
- setting conditions—the story will have as many episodes as knots in a piece of string, or it must reach a satisfactory conclusion in a given time, or it must use the words of popular songs or rhymes.

*Puppet stories.* Have children build a collection of hand puppets using socks, gloves, and paper sacks. They can then choose a hand puppet and tell a story using the voice of the puppet character.

*Readers Theatre stories.* Read a story during read aloud or shared reading time that children will enjoy reading again. In groups, they can reread the story to the class using simple props and actions that will add a theatrical dimension to the story. Make sure children are given rehearsal time before they perform their Readers Theatre piece for others. Poetry reading, class plays, and news stories also can be part of Readers Theatre.

Knowing the elements of good storytelling will give children insight into discussing and analyzing their own and others' storytelling. To assess children's speaking and listening abilities through storytelling, have children discuss their performances using the questions below. These provide useful feedback to the storyteller and will help children to understand how speaking and listening are essential parts of the storyteller's craft.

- Did listeners understand the plot?
- Were the characters clearly defined—did you feel you "knew" them?
- Could you imagine the place where this story happened? What did it look like? ·
- What mood was created by the storyteller? Did it match the story?
- What did the storyteller do and say to add to the storytelling? Did he or she use hand and body movements to add information? Did the storyteller change his or her voice to match the different characters? Did the storyteller repeat key phrases and other clues to help the audience predict what would happen next?

### Factual Oral Texts

Aside from storytelling, teachers can provide opportunities for talk using the conventions of a range of other oral texts, such as debate, extemporaneous speaking, and investigative reporting. Plan programs that reflect teaching intentions for developing talk by creating classroom experiences that will specifically address particular oral language text types. Ensure that children have the opportunity to explore and understand the conventions of an oral text before they are required to use it.

*Debating.* Even young children can debate issues using formal debating procedures in which the roles of the speakers and audience are defined clearly. Have students use the checklists in Figure 5 to guide their listening and have everyone take the role of the judge—you will guarantee good listening!

*Extemporaneous speaking.* Students can choose topics to speak on informally from a list of agreed-upon suggestions such as books I have read, hobbies, sports, pets, vacations, personal adventures and misadventures, movies I have seen, special occasions, places I have visited, or any special interests and activities. The format for these talks can be decided by the whole class, and procedures can be listed in the classroom as a reference. Use checklists like the one in Figure 6 to guide the observations children make about each other's talks and to ensure that feedback is positive and helpful.

| FIGURE 5 Debating checklist | | | | |
|---|---|---|---|---|
| TITLE OF THIS DEBATE: | | | | |
| Team *FOR* the argument | Speaker 1 | Speaker 2 | Speaker 3 | Speaker 4 |
| Could you hear what the speaker said? | | | | |
| Did you understand the speaker's points of view? | | | | |
| Did the speaker have enough information? | | | | |
| Was the speaker interesting? | | | | |
| SCORE | | | | |
| Team *AGAINST* the argument | Speaker 1 | Speaker 2 | Speaker 3 | Speaker 4 |
| Could you hear what the speaker said? | | | | |
| Did you understand the speaker's points of view? | | | | |
| Did the speaker have enough information? | | | | |
| Was the speaker interesting? | | | | |
| SCORE | | | | |

| TEAM PRESENTATION | TEAM *FOR* THE ARGUMENT | TEAM *AGAINST* THE ARGUMENT |
|---|---|---|
| Were the team's arguments reasonable? | | |
| Could you follow the team's arguments? | | |
| Did the team use facts to support their arguments? | | |
| Do you think their evidence was accurate? | | |
| Did the team present some facts and some opinion? | | |
| Was the team convincing? | | |
| Did the team present well? | | |
| SCORE | | |

**FIGURE 6**
**Listener's guide**

NAME:
Name of topic:

Why did you choose this topic?

| | a lot | a little | sometimes |
|---|---|---|---|
| I liked the way you helped your listeners by | | | |
| • starting with the first thing we needed to know and adding more | | | |
| • summarizing what you had said so far | | | |
| • pausing and checking that we understood | | | |
| • answering our questions | | | |
| I liked the way you | | | |
| • spoke clearly and with expression | | | |
| • made eye contact with us | | | |
| • varied your voice to say it better | | | |
| • used gestures | | | |

This is what I learned

• that is new:

• that helped me understand more about this subject:

GENERAL COMMENTS:

*Investigative reports.* Children enjoy talking about the investigations and school projects they have undertaken. Make the completion of their work an opportunity for celebration and sharing, and an opportunity for children to present information to the class. Make this an alternative to traditional written book reports and written comprehension questioning. Topics may be part of any curriculum area—e.g., children may report their scientific investigation, demonstrate how to build something, recount what they have learned about the history of their town, or explain the significance of national flags and emblems.

Many children do not know how to ask questions that are relevant and that will tell them what they want to know to research their investigations. Help them plan what questions they need to ask, and provide children with a questionnaire planner such as the one in Figure 7.

Planning investigations will give children a way to

- decide what they want to find out—what will be the relevant questions?
- write down their questions—what are possible answers?

---

**FIGURE 7**
**Questionnaire planner**

WHAT DO I WANT TO FIND OUT?
*I want to know about how Sunbury was 50 years ago and how it has changed.*

WHO WILL I ASK?
*I am going to ask my neighbor Irene, who has lived in Sunbury all her life.*

WHAT QUESTIONS WILL I NEED TO ASK?

| INITIAL QUESTIONS | POSSIBLE SUPPLEMENTARY QUESTIONS |
|---|---|
| *How long have you lived in Sunbury?* | *How many people lived here when you came to the town?*<br>*Did you live in this house?*<br>*What was in your street when you first arrived?* |
| *What was here then?* | *How many schools were here?*<br>*Were the same stores in the main street?*<br>*Were there supermarkets here then?* |
| *What changes have you seen?* | *What has changed in your street?*<br>*When did the bus service start?*<br>*When was the first Sunbury Festival?* |
| *Do you know what happened before you came?* | *Do you know anyone who lived here before you and who could tell me about then?* |
| *Do you have any photographs of Sunbury when you first arrived here?* | *Do you know where I can get more information?* |

• prepare for likely responses—what supplementary questions might I need to ask to get the particular information I need?

Talk with children to help them develop ways of investigating and finding out, and ways of keeping track of what they are doing and where they are going with their investigations.

Checklists provide clear pathways and are a record of conversations held and work completed. The project checklist in Figure 8 can be adapted to suit individual children and the types of investigations and projects they undertake. Use the information provided by their checklists to teach children to assess their own performance, and to use what they find to inform their future learning directions by comparing their goals and the current status of their work.

## Providing a Wider Audience for Speaking and Listening

To extend talk outside the classroom, teachers can arrange activities in which students use talk in various other settings for authentic purposes. Teachers might think about establishing a school "radio station" using the public address system and perhaps broadcasting at lunchtimes. This can be accomplished by assigning children to collect information about the day's news and upcoming events and having them present a daily news bulletin. Projects also could be developed by students using oral language media such as tapes, videos, and musical performances that could be shown in the larger community.

Arranging time for discussion groups in which current event issues can be aired and responses developed is a good way to encourage students to think about what they say and hear. Authentic and formal responses to these issues could be made outside the classroom and could include calling the local radio station to report about the issue on the air, preparing a speech for a school assembly, addressing parent and school community groups, or surveying class and community groups to assess public opinion. Each of these responses requires children to use the conventions of the oral language text specific to that audience and purpose.

*Authors' Day.* Set aside a day, perhaps each term, when children can read from their own writing and discuss what they have written with others. Make it a special celebration and invite parents, other class groups, and other teachers to attend. Arrange for the following:

• a special "authors' chair"

• a chairperson who is responsible for introducing each author and providing biographical information for the audience

• snacks and drinks to be served at the conclusion of the readings

| FIGURE 8 | | |
|---|---|---|
| **Project checkpoints** | | |
| Name: | | Name of project: |
| Checkpoint | Date | Conferences and Discussions |
| 1. Topic Planning:<br>  topic selected, planning sheet completed<br>  planning conference held with teacher | | |
| 2. Information Collection:<br>  list of references found (keep reference material title,<br>  author for bibliography)<br>  notes and summaries written | | |
| 3. Project Draft: completed<br>  edited by friend<br>  edited by teacher | | |
| 4. Project Layout: planned and drafted<br>  think about the information, headings,<br>  illustrations, diagrams, bibliography | | |
| 5. Project Publishing | | |
| 6. Reporting to Class | | |
| 7. Personal Evaluation:<br>  Two things that were successful are…<br><br>  The thing I will do differently next time is…<br><br>  I managed my time… | | |
| 8. Teacher Evaluation: | | |

Teachers can help children understand how to assess these performances by

- outlining the task—what exactly do we have to do and say here?
- giving help when it is needed
- providing opportunities to practice
- modeling assessment language
- discussing with children the other issues that may need to be considered

# Final Considerations for Teachers

Self-assessment is an important note on which to finish a chapter on how talk might be shaped and shared in a classroom. Teachers can assess the effectiveness of their own discourse by keeping in mind the following questions:

- Who controls discourse in my classroom?
- Who decides who speaks when and for how long?
- Who chooses the topics on which discussion will focus?
- Who does most of the talking? Who does most of the listening?
- Who asks the questions? Who gives the answers?
- Do questions have one answer or do I allow for multiple interpretations?
- Are questions asked for authentic purposes?
- Do I allow enough time for children to think about what they want to say and respond to what is said?
- Do I miss opportunities for children to learn through talk?
- Do children understand the language? How much should I allow for children whose first language is not English?
- Do I ask children to rephrase what others have said before they respond?
- Do I value all contributions? What do I praise, what do I deprecate?

# Conclusions

Effective speaking and listening in classrooms does not happen without planning, monitoring, and constantly attuning our program to the learning needs of children. Our curriculum documents, our term and weekly planners, and our daily schedules will reflect our teaching intentions for learning to speak and listen and learning about speaking and listening in our classrooms.

It is so important that the teacher demonstrates the purposes, contexts, and audiences for speaking and listening experiences in the classroom, ensuring that children understand what the tasks require of them and why they are performing them. Children should be invited to engage in tasks at their own entry points. It should be clear that the speaking and listening classroom tasks are directly integrated with other key learning areas and with the children's own development as articulate members of a society.

The teacher needs to step down from center stage. No longer can all speaking and listening be directed by and through the teacher. Different classroom management principles may need to be considered. The teacher and the children may need to negotiate, develop, document, and practice different ways of operating in the classroom. It may seem hard at times, especially at the beginning when ground rules are being established. But it is not too hard, because the rewards arc manifold. Enjoy.

## Suggested Reading

*First steps oral language resource book.* (1997). Victoria, Australia: Rigby Heinemann.

Hancock, J., & Leaver, C. (1994). *Major teaching strategies for English.* Victoria, Australia: The Australian Reading Association.

Mallan, K. (1991). *Children as storytellers.* Newtown, Australia: Primary English Teaching Association.

Morrow, L.M. (1990). *Literacy development in the early years* (3rd ed.). Boston: Allyn & Bacon.

National Council of Teachers of English. (1998, August). *Primary Voices K–6, 7*(1).

Rowe, G. (1989). *Let's talk.* Melbourne, Australia: Dellasta.

# Shaping Conversations: Young Children's Philosophical Thought

*Gloria Latham*

## The Backdrop

When my daughters were very young we would spend hours on end engaged in vocal duets while creating soundscapes (environmental sound scores). Eager to reclaim my own sense of wonder, I followed their first encounters with verbal play, using the pages of my journal to record their explorations and the myriad questions they posed.

> Why is my face on the front of my head?
>
> Does a fly know he's a fly?
>
> Who will die first, you or me?
>
> How did the world first start?
>
> What happens to a knot when you untie your shoe?

Their questions were philosophical in nature and stemmed from an inherent need to make sense of the world they inhabited. In response to their barrage of wondering, I would often toss the questions back, asking my daughters their opinions of the issues they queried. Without hesitation, they would talk through their tentative theories while employing metaphysical thinking. In response to the question, Why do we have wind and rain? my 2$^1/_2$-year-old daughter offered her own explanation:

> I like the sun the best. I don't like the rain cause it makes your pants fall down.
> It splash on my legs. I just don't like the wind. It makes your clothes fly away.
> The wind makes me breathe. I like the sun the best but it gets in my eyes.

When my older daughter was 4 years old she and her friend speculated about the first person in the world.

| Anya: | I saw a film about bear bones. |
| Tommy: | Well let me ask you this, who was the first bear? |
| Anya: | The first bear was a father. |
| Tommy: | It couldn't have been, the first bear was a mother, it had to be. |
| Anya: | Oh, no. The first bear was a dinosaur. |
| Anya & Tommy: | Of course! (Latham, 1996, p. 13) |

I marveled at my daughters' inquisitive minds and became intrigued by the ways in which they pieced together the known with the unknown. In my role as an educator, I have often felt that children's philosophical conversations were silenced in schools. Perhaps the suppression of wild, unstructured thoughts helps to explain why curiosity and wonder disappear in childhood only to resurface, for some individuals, much later in life. There is also good reason to believe that wondering ceases when young children are supplied with fixed answers to their questions. Research into classroom talk (Alexander, 1992; Hall & Martello, 1996; McManus, 1987) indicates that teachers take little notice of the everyday knowledge children bring with them into the classroom. If educators fail to value children as a rich resource, it follows that children will soon learn to devalue what they know as well.

Children are robust thinkers who need time to roam in the world of possibilities in order to acquire a sense of self and a sense of place. I was eager to discover how all children live in the world and to learn how the philosophical thoughts young children express could be preserved and further developed into adulthood. A sense of wonder is central to the notion of being of the world. Aristotle suggests that wonder is a response to the novelty of experience. As long as the world remains strange and paradoxical, wonder will not cease. Cobb (1977) discusses nature as inviting children to greater creativity and meaning, she believes that children's ecological sense is "basically aesthetic and infused with joy in the power to know and to be" (p. 23). This sense incites the mind to organize novel information. The genius of childhood and the child's sense of wonder is aroused as a response to life's mysteries.

The years between 2 and 7 are critical with respect to how children deal with the world around them. It is within this time period that children form "beliefs, biases, artistry, curiosity and a sense of self that carries them forward into adulthood" (Latham, 1996, p. 12). Matthews (1980) and Splitter and Sharp (1995) provide strong evidence of children's philosophical orientation. Very young children's questions often arise from their direct encounters with the world as they discover its mysteries. These children are thought to be precultural and the world before them is made comprehensible through sensory experience.

# The Cast

The ease with which my daughters constructed and narrated diverse world views through interactions with each other and the larger community led me to more formal learning about the young child as thinker and theory builder. Some 20 years later I decided to focus more closely on how young children experience the world. In order to capture their surprise and joy and the knowledge gained, I chose to work with children between 5 and 7 years of age. I conversed with four small groups of three to five children on a daily basis over a 4½-month period—engaging them in discussions, role plays, listening to music, composite drawings, and constructions of those aspects of the world that interested them. The children invited to participate were selected from a mix of age groups, abilities, cultures, and genders. Each group visit lasted about 70 minutes.

Through these extensive interactions I learned that young children's inquisitive minds and their need to make meaning allow them to develop spontaneous theories about the world that they then adjust over time. The young children frequently referred to their ideas as theories. They would begin by claiming, "This is just a theory but I believe…." Pavlov imagined theories as a set of wings. He felt they allowed man to soar to the heavens. But facts are like the atmosphere against which those wings must beat, and without them the soaring bird will surely plummet back to earth (Gibbons, 1955).

As children mature and acquire new knowledge they undergo changes in their theories of mind (Wellman, 1990). These provisional theories were apparent in my conversations with young children. They would begin discussing an issue with a strong conviction often borne of their direct experience with the world: "I believe, my opinion of it is, it happened like this, when I look up at the sky, my theory about it is…." However, their convictions often waned when another child in the group would disagree or merely present another position. For instance, David illustrated the vacillation of his beliefs about God stating, "Well I used to…well once I used to and then I decided I wouldn't but now I've decided I'm not sure about whether there is a God." Here was a child who was told by his parents that there was no God yet he played with a group of boys who believed in God and often prayed together. Sometimes David pretended to pray as well and he told the boys that he did believe in God, just so he could be part of their group.

Gopnik and Wellman (1992, 1994) and Gopnik and Meltzoff (1997) posit the notion that children are theory builders from a very young age, and that their development in the cognitive processes is identical to the cognitive processes developed in scientists (p. 3). Bartsch and Wellman (1995) call this notion the *theory theory*: "the theory that a child's understanding of persons and minds constitutes an everyday theory" (p. 161). They describe a child's theory of mind as a naive theory rather than a scientific one. It is known that children develop their intuitive theories of the world in "the context of a society that already has much knowledge of the world" (p. 24).

Central to this notion of theory building is that the information children build about the world is derived from sources of authority rather than direct evidence after their initial years. Very young children undergo a restructuring in their thinking that is analogous to theory shifts (Flavell, Flavell, Green, & Moses, 1993; Gopnik & Wellman, 1994; Perner, 1991; Wellman, 1990). An *intuitive theory* is a system of interrelated concepts that generates explanations and predictions in particular domains of experience. Gopnik and Meltzoff (1997) believe theories have structural properties of abstractness, coherence, causal relationships, and ontological commitment; and functional features of prediction, interpretation, and explanation. These assist children in making sense of their world. Gardner's (1993) findings suggest that children at ages 5 and 6 have already developed theories about the world in three areas:

- developed theories of matter

- developed theories of living things

- developed theories of mind that include a theory of self

These theories are continually being tested.

After a few conversations, I realized that young children's thinking does indeed resemble the structural and functional theories of adults as well as the wonder and speculation of artists and scientists. The theoretical stances children take and the recurring shifts in their notions are evidence of their openness to receiving, processing, and reconstructing new information. Children also seem willing to roam freely between the worlds of science and art. They describe what the world is like and also express what they believe is possible.

Establishing the young child as a robust thinker with capabilities of theory building allows me to describe the powerful role that oral language serves in the learning process. Through dialogical exchanges, children encounter otherness, and by its very nature their world is expanded. In this otherness, children are provided with an occasion to think about the potentials and limitations of their lives as they encounter differing cultures, genders, and voices (Huspek, 1997). Talking is an inherently social act allowing children time to bounce ideas off others, gain wisdom, and continually adjust their tenuous theories as they talk themselves into meaning. Silence is not the absence of talk but rather a means to liberate thought. Oral language fosters contemplation and greater attention to the area under discussion. By organizing conversations in small groups, all children's voices have an opportunity to be heard and the powerful thoughts that are generated can remain malleable and fluid. This is essential for children to be able to explore life's mysteries while continually shifting and expanding their theories. Curiosity and wonder are preserved, explored, and valued.

Ongoing conversations also create a community of inquiry driven by the spring of wonderment. Stories are heard and passed on, and rituals are created such as the passing of the philosopher's stone. As a teacher-researcher, I am well aware that I would never have been offered the deep thoughts of these children had they merely been asked to write them down.

## The Setting

In order to hold conversations with the children I was provided with a small room in which to work. It held a rectangular table and enough chairs to seat five people comfortably. The room kept out most exterior sound and became an ideal space for our project. It seems teachers in school settings go to great lengths to design and create reading/writing and computer spaces in their classroom, yet spend little time thinking about environments that help foster rich and fruitful discussions. I wanted the environment to resemble the Sunday dinners of my childhood, where relatives assembled and took their seats at a table spread with food and books while engaging in rich conversation. In the little room I hoped that ideas would be our nourishment. I covered the table with large sheets of paper and brought a box of colored pens and pencils to every discussion. I soon learned about the power of pictorial representations as a stimulus for the development of critical thinking, and for explaining and drawing links among ideas. Diagrams, drawings, and maps were constructed individually and collaboratively, and these helped to inform spoken thoughts. When Peter had difficulty making his thoughts about the life cycle clear to the other group members, I suggested he draw a diagram to explain what he meant. Together we created the world and colored it in with wondering.

The desire to work in small-group settings was fostered by my strong belief that the knowledge most worth knowing is brought about dialogically. Dialogical learning is an exchange between people seeking mutual agreement and understanding (Brogan & Brogan, 1995). (See the discussion of Bakhtin in Chapter 1, page 3 for more about dialogue.) Rather than view the child as an active scientist constructing knowledge on his or her own, making sense of the world can be viewed as a social process within a cultural and historical context (Bruner, 1987). As such, meaning becomes a coconstruction. Geertz (1975) reminds us that

> Human thought is consummately social; social in its origins, social in its functions, social in its forms, social in its applications. At base thinking is a public activity—its natural habitat is the house-yard, the marketplace, the town square. (p. 360)

The children were accustomed to working in multiage group settings and their ease and acceptance of each other's viewpoints was apparent. I worked at establishing a feeling of trust that would unite us in thoughtfulness (Bollnow, 1989).

Group members extend and are challenged by each other's ideas. Young children, in concert with others, talk themselves into meaning, accommodate for other people's ways of making meaning, and coconstruct meaning between them. The tone that is set at the start of a conversation often determines the very nature of the ideas that will be created. As the children had a sympathetic and interested audience for their ideas, they felt eager to share and listen to the ideas of others. A young child would often look up from her drawing and stare into the face of a speaker with a look of great respect. It seemed as though it was the first time the listener had recognized the speaker as a knowledgeable and respected thinker. I overheard one child proudly showing her mother our room. "See," she said, "this is the little room where we talk about the world."

## The Roles

At times, I encouraged the children to come to our room in the role of scientists, philosophers, reporters, or Earth spirits. They slipped in and out of these roles as easily as they changed the topics of conversation. They also easily adopted the discourse of the particular character. For instance, David began his talk as a scientist by stating, "My name is Dr. David and today I will be talking about how Pluto became. If you want to ask any questions or anything afterwards, or maybe if you're somewhere else listening to this you can get me on my phone number…OK, let's begin." Often, even the children's discussion following the talk was in role. I asked, "Well, Dr. David, do you think it's possible that Pluto may have been formed in another way?" David replied, "Well, yes, that is possible…. That's a very good idea actually." Stephen began his talk as philosopher by stating, "I am going to tell you about something long, long, long ago about how the earth became." Laura talked from her position as a spirit, announcing, "I am the water spirit. I am the spirit of all gods and evil things…." Halliday (1978) reminds us that as children talk they also learn more about their role as speakers. As the children always had an audience for their thoughts, they took on roles and employed a variety of language functions in order to persuade, inform, and entertain their listeners.

These roles allowed the children the freedom to wear the persona of another in order to evoke empathy by adopting a new position. Cohen and Manion (1980) discuss the use of role–play in educational research. *Role-play* is defined as "participation in simulated social situations that are intended to shed light on the role/rule contexts governing 'real'–life social episodes" (Cohen & Manion, 1980, p. 252). As play is the business of childhood, the child comes to understand the world by becoming the world. Chukovsky (1962) asserts that children create alternative worlds in play not to avoid reality but rather to confirm their knowledge of it. While in role, I treated the children as experts, being respectful of their knowledge and deeply interested in their speculation.

# Rehearsals

Young children have some difficulty thinking inside their heads and often stutter, stammer, and employ hesitations as they explore ideas in order to construct and organize meaning. The children in my group often backed up and circled an idea to ultimately snare it. One child, while exploring the origins of man, stated,

> I think um, I think that when I think about um the world like sometimes I think about…well sometimes I think about um like um kind of like um, it's a bit hard to understand, but sometimes when um I'm really interested in something like um I keep on asking questions like what really happened in the olden days? Like I kind of think that it (the first person) was a gorilla and it changed into a person.

Williams (1975) is convinced that stammering, stuttering, and silences are necessary for children as they struggle to articulate monumental issues about the world. I began to think of stammering, stuttering, and silence as "thought's space" and worked to preserve this space as sacred ground belonging to the speaker. Often the young children's thoughts were not caught and remained in the air unresolved. Said Laura, "I can't even understand my words because Adam was the first person in the world and how did they make him?" Some children returned to a previous thought after the discussion had moved on, as illustrated in the following student comment:

> I'm still thinking about those first people who came alive first and the first person was Bubba Jesus when he married one of the cherubs and they made some children and then they (the children) became grown-ups and they made a girl and boy and it keeps going on, girls then boys.

As the children seldom composed in their heads, they needed a great deal of time and patience from their listeners to allow them to arrive at their ideas.

Young children are quite capable of taking thought beyond the literal, and these children's use of figurative language appeared to assist their understanding as well as mine. Metaphoric thinking was often used in their spontaneous speech with others. One of the children, Jules, used figurative language to comment on his drawing, saying "Look, look at Japan, it looks like one of those Picasso paintings." Peter described the earth's movement as being "like a merry-go round or like it's hitting like a wind chime…." While explaining gravity to the group, Laura had stated that, "Wherever oxygen is, gravity comes with it." When I asked her what she meant by that she replied, "Buy one, get one free." Metaphoric thinking was an active part of the children's story making.

As I worked to understand the children's thoughts, I realized that a great deal of the meaning was contained in their gestures, facial expressions, and body language. I understood the importance of acquiring information beyond their verbal and artistic responses. In order to compensate, I mentally recorded areas such as how the children entered the room, their facial expressions during the discussion, and their level of involvement in the issues. I recorded these impressions in my journal directly following each discussion. These anecdotal records assisted understanding of this nonverbal meaning-making. Later, when listening to the tapes I found they were hollow without the faces and voices of the children. Yet listening to the tapes over and over again allowed me to hold the children in my memory, and the transcripts of their words became similar to cinematic documentaries played back to me. At times the images and voiced thoughts were contradictory. For instance, Warren would express highly sophisticated ideas about the world and then suck his thumb while he listened to his peers. Steven, who explained the beginning of electricity, was drawing and labeling a model when he asked me how to spell *there*. The other children looked up in disbelief. I had to keep reminding myself that I was in the company of children who were 5 to 7 years of age. There were a great many things to come to terms with while trying to understand how children live in the world.

## The Conversation

Rich and fruitful conversations cannot be crafted. They are generated quite spontaneously by people being in the world together. Just as stories grow from stories, ideas are borne of ideas that are communicated among people. Conversations are transitory, multifocused, and self-regulating. It is the "everydayness" of conversations that make them useful to us.

While in our room, the topics of conversation grew out of the children's "everyday" curiosity. On the first visit with each group I asked them what they wanted to know about the world. As their wondering tumbled forth, we created a list of questions that they attempted to answer.

How did the world come to be?

What were the first living things on earth?

How did the dinosaurs disappear?

What's in the world?

Is the earth alive?

When a question was no longer of interest it was abandoned and new directions were sought. Sometimes the conversation would roam wild while at other times it was tamed and shaped by its participants. A philosopher's stone was brought in and passed around as each child spoke. It allowed the holder the right to be heard, and the children would rub it repeatedly to bring forth ideas. Within the first few days of conversing, it became apparent that most of the children's thoughts were shared as narratives. They would begin, "Well, it all happened like this…. Okay, let's begin the story…. Once upon a time, millions and millions of years ago…."

Educators have long recognized the value of reading and telling stories to young children, yet it is only in recent years that recognition has been paid to the stories children tell. Childhood is the time when children learn who they are and what they will become, and narratives help to socialize them and allow them to forge new relationships. Children are quite naturally storied beings who become the stories they tell. There is in narrative the means to organize events and make sense of them. Through stories, children are able to enter and explore other worlds beyond direct experience in order to evoke empathy. One group of children established a whole set of narrative practices during the conversations. For instance, Warren was explaining what the world would be like in the year 2220. As he finished he said, "And that's the end of Chapter One." Suddenly the children in the group's eyes glistened with new light as they sought to create the next chapters of the world's story. After six long chapters had been related and connected, Patrick asked, "Please can I end it, can I end it?" The others responded, "You're ending it, go ahead." With delight, Patrick said, "And one day all the troubles vanished from Earth. The end."

## Moving Beyond the Script

While listening to the children tell their stories, there were times I felt certain they were speaking the scripts of significant others: "God created people because he was lonely," "The stars are all the people who have died," "The rain only falls on the rich people's land." Stereotypes children adopt from parents, extended family members, peers, the society at large, and the media play a significant role in early theory building. Gardner (1993) extends the notion of scripts in discussing young children's theory building. He believes scripts are necessary in order to provide children with demonstrations of social situations such as the script of the family trip, the birthday party, and the first lost tooth. It was my intention to take the children beyond the use of scripts, as scripts seal ways of knowing and deny children opportunity to roam in uncertainty. To challenge the scripts they adopted, I questioned their statements in some depth. For instance, most of the children readily stated that we do not fall off the world because gravity holds us down. Because this may have been a script expressed but not understood, it was necessary to try and discover their understanding of gravity. I returned to the idea on several occasions and asked the children to draw a diagram and show me how gravity operated. Some of the drawings helped me to go beyond the words uttered.

# The Director's Role

The teacher wields great power in shaping children's discourse. For instance, if I asked the children the size of the earth, their conversation tended to proceed as scientific discourse. Yet, when asking them whether or not the earth was alive, the children's responses were far more speculative and exploratory. Even though they decided the direction of the conversation, my questioning determined a great deal.

Speech rises out of silence and returns to silence (Bollnow, 1982). It needs to be listened to. In order to understand what it is like to be in the world with young children I had to learn to engage in active listening. A great deal of my data gathering was concerned with improving ways of listening, because if I was to enter the world of the children it was necessary to concentrate fully and open my mind to what was before me. Graves (1990) explains that he listens with "two ears: to the words of children speaking and to [my] own inner voice…" (p. 83). As I worked with the children in the little room and listened repeatedly to the tapes, I worked at listening in this dually focused way. I listened to their words and beneath their words. I listened for pain and joy in the voices of the children. I also worked hard at listening and becoming aware of the numerous voices within me, and what my voices brought to the community of thinkers.

Van Manen (1990) discusses different kinds of silences. The first is *literal silence*, the absence of speech. Out of these silences often comes the most reflective thought. The second type of silence is *epistemological*, which is when the individual faces something she is incapable of describing. Here lies tacit knowing, which is knowing more than we can articulate—the silence of the unspeakable. Third, there is *ontological silence*—the silence of life itself. Bollnow (1989) describes this as being in the presence of truth. It was necessary to try to listen for all these silences and discover the treasures hidden under the surface of spoken thought.

As well as employing active listening, I needed to know when to step in and move the conversation and when to let it run freely. Most of the time a group member stepped in to follow up a point or to try and clarify something for himself or herself. For instance, Steven was explaining how the planet earth formed:

> Millions and millions of years ago, before mankind, the earth was all cracked up. And what I believe is that the cracks pulled each thing together cause the sun was on one side and the moon was on the other side so the moon and stars were moving towards the sun and what I believe is when those stars exploded it glued a magnetic force to the cracks and out of time, these cracks are coming back and I don't know why but I would appreciate it if they would just go.

Daniel then stepped in to comment on Steven's idea.

> I don't understand because the only place that mostly has cracks is the desert…so I would say, my expression of it is that the cracks are just caused

by the fire in the earth. Sometimes it rumbles and there comes a small crack in the ground but it's mostly in the desert.

Both children were deep in thought, and they moved the conversation back and forth to explore the endless possibilities.

# The Performance

Implied in the sentiments expressed above is the need for a classroom to be a place of inquiry—a thoughtful community. Teachers and children can set up circles of inquiry where, in small groups and with the whole class, all participants are encouraged to generate thoughtful talk.

Seat children around tables covered in paper where they can draw their ideas, jot notes, and build mind and body maps. Engage them in role plays where they don a lab coat as a scientist or follow their journey as a group of explorers. This will generate a symphony of purposeful talk—furthered, circled, and sometimes snared—as well as expressions of puzzlement, stillness, and excitement in a flurry of movement. Tentative, fragile theories will alter in midstream as the thoughts of others alter them, and rich, expansive language appropriate to the speaker will sing forth.

Teachers need to engage learners in fruitful discussions that express curiosity about the world. It is important to foster an atmosphere of respect for each other's ideas, which will assist in elevating children's language, deepening their thought processes, and helping to clarify their ideas. Teachers should allow the pregnant silence to remain in the air untouched until the next wave of ideas take flight.

When all this is accomplished, teachers will hear meaning being made among their students. "Aha!" the children will joyously exclaim, "Now I understand!"

# Postscript

Building conversation in the classroom is a means toward furthering young children's critical thinking and building a thoughtful community of learners. However, establishing an atmosphere under which this community functions effectively involves a complex set of forces. The Goertzels (1962) wrote a seminal text in which they investigated the childhoods of 400 eminent adults in order to ascertain the factors that contributed to their later development. The authors found that as children, these adults had been given a great deal of freedom to make their own choices. As well, they were allowed time to play and solve problems, to tinker, and to make messes. Instead of being trivialized, play was encouraged and valued.

The children I conversed with were allowed time to tinker with ideas. No matter what thoughts were expressed, or how long it took to express them, they were developed and deepened in an attempt to clarify the ideas for the speaker and the listeners. Ideas were valued by the group members in an environment of trust. The young children were treated as experts, and they were repeatedly told that the theories they espoused could not be wrong. They were happily roaming in the realm of possibilities. As well as feeling free to express thoughts without ridicule, the children were encouraged to discuss topics that were of immense interest to them. They were engaged in authentic learning experiences and were provided with authentic assessment. The knowledge and understandings they brought to the conversations were acknowledged. All this was necessary to sustain the conversations and produce a coconstruction of new form and meaning.

It is in their formative years in which young children's wondering is either ignited or extinguished. To help young children continue to see the world as paradoxical and strange is to keep curiosity and exploration alive for the rest of their lives.

## References

Alexander, R. (1992). *Policy and practice in primary education.* London: Routledge.
Bartsch, K., & Wellman, H.M. (1995). *Children talk about the mind.* New York: Oxford University Press.
Bollnow, O.F. (1989). The pedagogical atmosphere: The perspective of the child. *Phenomenology and Pedagogy, 7,* 12–36.
Brogan, B.R., & Brogan, W.R. (1995). The Socratic questioner: Teaching and learning in a dialogical classroom. *The Educational Forum, 59,* 288–296.
Bruner, J. (1986). *Actual minds, possible worlds.* Cambridge, MA: Harvard University Press.
Chukovsky, K. (1962). *From two to five.* Berkeley, CA: University of California Press.
Cobb, E. (1977). *The ecology of imagination in childhood.* London: Routledge & Kegan Paul.
Cohen, L., & Manion, L. (1980). *Research methods in education.* New York: Routledge.
Flavell, J.H., Flavell, E.R., Green, F.L., & Moses, l.J. (1993). *Cognitive development.* Englewood Cliffs, NJ: Prentice Hall.
Gardner, H. (1993). *The unschooled mind.* London: Fontana Press.
Geertz, C. (1975). *The interpretation of cultures.* New York: Basic Books.
Gibbons, J. (Ed.). (1955). *Selected works* (S. Belsky, Trans.). Moscow: Foreign Languages Publishing House.
Goertzel, M., & Goertzel, R. (1962). *Cradles of eminence.* Boston: Little, Brown.
Gopnik, A., & Meltzoff, A.N. (1997). *Words, thoughts and theories.* Cambridge, MA: MIT Press.
Gopnik, A., & Wellman, H.M. (1992). Why the child's theory of mind really is a theory. *Mind and Language, 7,* 145–171.
Gopnik, A., & Wellman, H.M. (1994). The theory theory. In L.A. Hirschfield & S.A. Gelman (Eds.), *Mapping the mind: Domain specificity in cognition and culture* (pp. 257–293). Hillsdale, NJ: Erlbaum.
Graves, D. (1990). *Discover your own literacy.* Portsmouth, NH: Heinemann.
Hall, N., & Martello, J. (1996). *Listening to children think.* London: Hodder & Stoughton.
Halliday, M.A.K. (1978). *Language as social semiotic.* London: Edward Arnold.
Huspek, M. (Ed.). (1997). *Transgressing discourses: Communication and the voice of other.* New York: State University of New York Press.

Latham, G. (1996). Fostering and preserving wonderment. *Australian Journal of Early Childhood, 21*(1), 6–12.

Matthews, G. (1980). *Philosophy and the young child*. Cambridge, MA: Harvard University Press.

McManus, M. (1987). I said hands up. *The Educational Times Supplement*. p. 10.

Perner, J. (1991). *Understanding the representational mind*. Cambridge, MA: MIT Press.

Splitter, L., & Sharp, A. (1995). *Teaching for better thinking*. Melbourne, Australia: The Australian Council for Educational Research.

vanManen, M. (1990). *Researching lived experience: Human science for an action sensitive pedagogy*. Albany, NY: State University of New York Press.

Williams, W.C. (1975). *The knack of survival*. New Brunswick, NJ: Rutgers University Press.

Wellman, H.M. (1990). *The child's theory of mind*. Cambridge, MA: Bradford Books/MIT Press.

## For Further Reading

Bjorklund, D.F. (1989). *Children's thinking: Developmental function and individual differences*. Belmont, CA: Brookes/Coles.

Coles, R. (1992). *The spiritual life of children*. London: HarperCollins.

Jones, P. (1996). *Talking to learn*. Newtown, New South Wales, Australia: Primary English Teaching Association.

Tizard, B., & Hughes, M. (1984). *Young children learning: Talking and thinking at home and in school*. London: Fontana.

# Creating Space for Sharing in the Writing Circle

*Frank Serafini, Rebecca Willey, and Jennifer Funke*

Jennifer, the teacher, sits on the floor of the classroom propped up against a short table in the center of the room. The soft hum of children talking fills the air. She is listening attentively to a heated discussion about the characteristics of *Pokémon*, a television series that two boys had been watching. Alex tells Eddie that it is his story and that if he wants to give his character extra powers he can because he is the author. Eddie replies, "Yeah, you're the author but Pokémon can't fly like that."

Walking past the computer station near the back of the room, Sofia, a young girl from Bosnia, is reading aloud from the Dr. Seuss book *Green Eggs and Ham*. She sees me (Frank) watching her and looks up from her reading for a moment to smile and wave. Slowly, she passes by, continuing to read aloud from the book, "That Sam, I am. That Sam, I am. I do not like that Sam, I am."

Behind me, two more boys sit at "the illustrating table." They are drawing with markers, practicing their illustrations for an upcoming picture book they are publishing. As he rummages through the plastic box of markers, José tells Billy that none of the black markers are working. Upset, he goes back to pawing through the box in order to find one black marker with some life left in it.

After about 45 minutes, Jennifer calls out, "OK! Let's wrap it up!" Students slowly get up and start milling around in front of the writing cubbies, putting some of their papers into their cubby drawers. Other students keep their papers in their hands and walk to the front of the room, finding places on the perimeter of a rectangular piece of carpet that has been placed on the floor. After a few minutes, the children are seated and talking quietly as they wait for someone to start the next activity. Jennifer calls over to one boy standing near the wastebasket, "Chris, let's go! We are waiting for you."

Chris throws some papers into the basket as he replies, "I'm coming!" He squeezes between two boys who grumble as they make room for the newcomer.

Jennifer, looking over at the writer's sign-up sheet, says, "OK. José you're up next."

José, looking startled, replies, "That must have been from a long time ago, I don't remember signing up, I don't have anything I want to read today."

Jennifer says, "All right," and looks back at the sign up sheet, "Melissa, you're up next."

The class giggles because Melissa is already standing up holding her papers. Jennifer turns to see her and says, "Oh, I guess you are ready. Good for you." The class laughs quietly as Melissa waits for the group to settle before she begins to speak. She smiles and looks around at the group from over the top of the wrinkled papers she holds firmly in her hand. Slowly, in a steady voice, she tells the group, "Well, this story is about dogs. I am reading this because I need more ideas."

The children are sitting quietly, looking at Melissa. They are sitting in what has come to be known as the "writer's circle." Melissa looks away from the group and back down at her paper as she begins to read her story aloud to the group.

"There are all kinds of dogs like a Chow, and a Golden Retriever and a Labrador, or a Poodle or a Sheepdog or a Chihuahua and Dalmatian...Bulldog...Pit bull...Husky. Dogs like to chew on my shoes and many objects. Dogs bury bones. Some dogs have long tails and some dogs have short tails. Puppies are cute but when they get bigger they can make a mess. Only the girl dogs have babies."

When she finishes, she stares quietly at the class and a smile slowly spreads across her face as the children begin to applaud. She looks around the circle to see if anyone has raised his or her hand. One girl has raised her hand and Melissa calls out her name, "McKenzie."

McKenzie says, "You should put in commas."

From the other side of the circle Vince yells out, "You don't know if she put in commas or not."

Jennifer gives him a stern look and he quickly stops and raises his hand, but Melissa is listening to McKenzie.

McKenzie begins again, "Jennifer told me how to put in commas last week, I can show you."

Jennifer says, "OK, wait a second." She stands up and walks over to the white board just outside the circle of children. She pulls it over so that most of the children can see it, and she tells Melissa to read her story exactly the way she wrote it. Some of the children turn around so they can see the board.

Jennifer writes what Melissa dictates to her on the white board with a blue marker. When Melissa finishes, Jennifer asks McKenzie to come up to the white board. The other students sit quietly and watch as McKenzie takes a red marker and begins to make changes to the sentence, putting in several commas and taking out some *and a's* and a few *or a's*. When she finishes making the changes to the series of words, she adds an "and a" before the name of the last dog.

Jennifer stands up and asks Melissa to read the sentence on the white board with the changes that McKenzie has made. Melissa reads it out loud and begins to nod her head, seeming to indicate that she understands and approves of the changes.

Jennifer turns to the group and says, "Can anyone tell Melissa why this sounds better?" Armand raises his hand and Jennifer calls on him.

Armand says, "It sounds better 'cause there aren't so many *ands*."

At this point, Jennifer says that Armand is right and talks about this idea with the class. She goes on to explain about how commas are used with words in a series. When she is done explaining this concept, she turns to McKenzie and tells her, "You remembered this from the time we spent working on it together. Good job." McKenzie smiles.

Melissa says, "I think I understand what to do now. I'll work it some more when we have writing tomorrow."

Jennifer says, "Great! That's all we have time for today. Line up for recess please."

The children quickly jump up and form a line at the door, grabbing playground balls and jump ropes as they file out of the room.

The purpose of the preceeding vignette is to help the reader vicariously experience the classroom environment that existed in a primary, multiage classroom in an inner-city elementary school in the southwestern United States. It was within this classroom context that we focused our observations and discussions on the talk and interactions that occurred during the writing circle.

Jennifer and Rebecca, both teachers in a multiage classroom setting, supported what may be described as a student-centered, whole language orientation (Edelsky, Altwerger, & Flores, 1991). Students were involved in choosing their writing topics (Atwell, 1998), assumed responsibility for the direction of their writing projects (Calkins, 1994), and chose stories to publish (Harste, Short, & Burke, 1988). The teachers focused on a process approach to writing (Graves, 1983), and learning was viewed as a social, constructive process (Vygotsky, 1978). In these two classrooms, writing instruction was organized into a workshop approach (Atwell, 1998), allowing students to choose their writing topics and proceed through the writing process to eventually publish their pieces of writing. At the end of these writing workshop time blocks, students gathered in the writing circle to share their writing and receive feedback for their efforts.

Frank was the Title I teacher in this elementary school, where the Title I position had been reorganized to allow him to work in classrooms as a "collaborative consultant" (Jaeger, 1996, p. 622), rather than working in a pull-out model with individual students. Frank was able to spend at least an hour a day observing these writing circles. As classroom teachers, we believe that our own observations and reflections should be the basis of our decisions concerning curriculum. Because of this, we spent time collecting observations and discussing our notes in order to make decisions concerning the structure and processes of our writing circles. Questions arose about the purpose of having students share their writing in the writing circle, the effects of these oral interactions on the student's writing, and the effects of various teacher interventions.

In this chapter we attempt to reveal some of the insights we have constructed about the nature of teacher–student interactions in the writing circle. We will focus on the oral interactions between teacher and student, and between students, realizing of course that these interactions involve more than just words to convey meaning. How things are said, one's body language, classroom context, and mannerisms carry meaning as well as the oral transcripts. Our goal is to provide classroom teachers with an understanding of the ways in which teachers can use the oral interactions during writing circle to support individual students' writing processes.

# The Writing Circle

## Theoretical Foundations

Writing circle has been referred to as *share circle, author's chair,* or *publisher's chair* depending on the researcher or author doing the writing. This activity has been alleged to support students' writing, foster interactions among student writers, create classroom community, allow teachers an opportunity to demonstrate writing techniques, and provide the necessary response for writers to improve their writing (Calkins, 1994). This sharing in writing circle is primarily oral in nature—a student reads his or her piece aloud and other students respond orally.

Writer's workshop was first developed as a model that mirrored the way "real" writers progressed through a piece of writing (Graves, 1983). This model was then redesigned to support teachers' structure of the writing process in the elementary writing classroom. One of the key components is the need for writers to share their writing and to receive feedback on their efforts. This sharing of student writing is done primarily through talk. It is this talk that is the foundation for supporting students' learning and sharing in the writing circle.

## Assessing the Writing Circle

Due to the contextual nature of the oral interactions during a writing circle, more formalized methods of assessment, such as standardized tests, are not consistent with our needs as classroom teachers and our purposes for understanding these interactions. Because of the limitations of these standardized assessments, we looked to more authentic means of assessing students' development as writers and the oral interactions that supported this development. As classroom teachers we used observations, anecdotal records, and occasional audio recordings to gather information to inform our practice.

Realizing that we needed a practical method of assessing the growth of individual students' writing, we struggled with developing a form or checklist that would allow us to gather information and facilitate the writing circle at the same time. We have used observational (anecdotal) record-keeping as an instrument for gathering information in our classrooms since we began teaching. As children were sharing their stories during the writing circle, Rebecca and Jennifer would keep a journal available for recording their thoughts and observations. Because Frank was not required to facilitate the discussions during the writing circle, he was able to take more elaborate notes and to observe the teacher's role in the writing circle more closely. We used these journal notes and observational data as a starting point for our discussions during our teacher dialogue groups. Reflecting on the information we gathered and sharing these thoughts in our discussions helped us to organize the writing circle and make changes that supported the interactions among students and the development of their writing.

# Assertions

Teacher–student interactions can be represented and analyzed in various ways. We chose to focus on the following assertions about teacher and student talk and the social interactions that took place in the writing circle. Our assertions are grouped into two categories: first, a focus on the teacher's talk and second, a focus on the student's talk.

Teacher Focus

1. The teacher uses the oral and written interactions during the writing circle to demonstrate the craft and mechanics of writing.
2. The teacher responds to the talk during the writing circle to facilitate the discussion in the actual writing circle itself.
3. The teacher uses the interactions, primarily oral in nature, during writing circle to help children understand the procedures of the writing workshop and the steps in the writing process.

Student Focus

1. Students refer to literature and other classroom "texts" when sharing and talking about their writing.
2. Students use talk during the writing circle to create their definitions of what it means to be a writer/author.
3. Students view the writing circle as an oral reading event as well as a writing event.
4. Student talk demonstrates noticeable differences between the type of talk concerning the actual content of the story and the talk that focused on the mechanics of the story.

## Assertions Expanded: Teacher Focus

*Teachers use the oral and written interactions during writing circle to demonstrate craft and mechanics of writing.*

This assertion is based on the premise that teaching in writing workshop is more of a response to students' efforts than an activity preplanned and directed by the teacher. Teachers observe what happens in the writing circle and based on their knowledge of the writing process they intervene to directly explain, or bring to the student's conscious awareness, a writing concept. This is done primarily through oral conversation.

Students in writing workshop work on pieces of writing at their own level, at their own pace, and on topics they choose for themselves. Because of this, the teacher needs to understand the writing process itself, and the individual student's writing abilities, in order to decide when to intervene and when to stay out of the discussion. In the following excerpt from an interview with one of the teachers in the study, the teacher discusses her use of the interactions during the writing circle to support the teaching of a specific craft of writing.

Jennifer refers to the episode described in the opening vignette in discussing how she decides to intervene in the writing circle.

> Another purpose I have [for intervening] is the idea that through the writing circle, students are able to share their ideas about what sounds like proper sentence structure or grammar. "Ain't" isn't a word, you can use the phrase "*went* on the elevator" instead of "*goed* [sic] on the elevator." So in a way they become more critical of each other in "that just didn't sound right." This falls in line with basically sentence structure, rules of grammar, but yet, it's not being taught directly, where at times it is. At times when there is an opportunity for me to interject, I'll say "OK, you noticed that something doesn't sound quite right and you seem to be struggling with ways to make it sound right, here's some ideas." In our language, when we have four names in a row, instead of saying "and Chelsea and Zachary and Nick and so and so," we just use commas to separate those and so that's when it becomes an opportunity for a minilesson to teach some of the rules of the [English] language, but that really only comes out when it's needed in the writer's circle. And that's a fine line for me as a teacher to walk as to when do I interject and impose the rules of the language and when do I allow them to discover and inquire with each other about "You know I *goed* on the elevator doesn't sound right" and even if they don't know what word does go in there, they know "I *goed*" doesn't sound right.

In this excerpt, Jennifer is making conscious decisions about when to intervene and when not to intervene. She is also trying to decide which grammar elements and elements of writing craft she wants to teach or bring to conscious attention. This is an example of the teacher using the writing circle to help children understand the structures of the English language and the craft of writing. It is a deliberate intervention on her part, based on her perceived needs of the children and her understanding of written language and the writing process.

The teacher and students in Jennifer's classroom are focusing on the conventions of talk that they know from being speakers of a specific English language dialect. Students and teacher are referring to the implicitly held understandings about the syntactic nature of oral language and how it connects to our written language. They are using this form of talk to support their writing.

Another quote from the same interview helps to explain why Jennifer chose to intervene with Melissa when she did.

I chose that one [intervention or minilesson] with Melissa, because of where she is "at" in her development, she needs to know how to put commas in her stories. I might not expect someone else to understand how to use commas yet. I would expect them to have the "ands," because that is where they are at [an individual child's language or writing development]. But she [Melissa] has had enough exposure to commas and used commas in other places, that I felt that was something that she needed to come around to…and the other part of it was there are other children that are going through that "comma thing" right now and I thought that this would reinforce them. Sometimes, I am the one up there [in front of the group] showing them how it works on the white board, but knowing that McKenzie had just done that [worked on commas in a series of words], I thought it would be good to have one of Melissa's peers explain that…and I wanted her [McKenzie] to verbalize it because I think it is important for the children to be able to explain themselves and to hear explanations from each other, because they are often times different or they connect in a different way to when I am speaking to them. So I just saw that as an opportunity to bring her in, but I chose to stop there because I knew that Melissa needed to be moving on to that [referring to commas in her writing] and there were enough others right now that have been "toying" with commas and I thought that was a good thing to go with.

Jennifer explains that interventions were done in the context of the writing circle and were a calculated response to the writing of the students. The classroom teacher has different expectations for each child and makes decisions about when to directly teach an aspect of writing and when not to intervene. The question is not about direct or indirect instruction, but about when to "directly" teach and when to let children come to the ideas on their own. These decisions are based on the teacher's knowledge of the children in her class and her knowledge of the writing process.

The interventions in this study were primarily oral in nature and became a specific type of talk that the teachers used to promote writing and understanding of language conventions. This type of talk did not ordinarily take place in other settings during the day, but was primarily focused on the connections between written language and oral language conventions. The teachers used these opportunities to demonstrate to the whole group concepts or conventions that they chose to introduce. This type of teacher intervention was a response to a perceived need that the teachers identified and then acted on.

*The teacher responds to the talk during the writing circle to facilitate the discussion in the actual writing circle itself.*

This assertion originally came to our attention because of the continued use of the phrases "I expect…" and "You know it is your responsibility to…" in interviews and field observations. It became quite clear that there were certain expectations for social interactions, for classroom behavior, and for the procedures used during the writing workshop—and during the writing circle in particular—that the teachers in this study communicated to their students. These expectations were conveyed primarily through teacher talk and became another type of discourse that the teacher drew from to support student writing and classroom interactions. These expectations developed over the course of the year and the teachers seemed to be the principal enforcers of these expectations. The writing circle was the primary context for communicating these expectations.

For example, Jennifer and Rebecca expected their students to sit and listen to the speaker during the writing circle. In order to facilitate this expectation, the teachers would often intervene and explain what they felt the appropriate behavior should be during writing circle. These expectations were usually discussed in the context in which they appeared and were clearly and directly articulated to the students.

*The teacher uses the interactions, primarily oral in nature, during writing circle to help children understand the procedures of the writing workshop and the steps in the writing process.*

This assertion became apparent because of the constant referrals to what students were expected to do next after they shared their stories. On many occasions the teachers asked the students what they planned to do next with their piece, and advised them to go back later in the day, or the next day, and work on their piece of writing. Instead of explaining to each child individually what he or she needed to do next, these teachers would often use the context of the writing circle to intervene and explain what was expected. The teachers often called on individual students in the group to help explain to the other students what they should do next.

The following transcript from one of the writing circle discussions illustrates an interaction between the group and one individual student. In this transcript the student is not prepared as the group and the teacher expect. What ensues is an interesting example of the high level of expectations in this classroom.

Teacher (Jennifer): Billy isn't here today (reading from the writing circle sign-up list) so…Christopher, you're next.

Christopher: I lost mine.

Shane
(to Christopher): Then what did you sign up for then?

Jennifer: Please raise your hand if you have something you want to say. (The group was starting to all talk at once to Christopher.)

Shane: I can see a lot of writing in your cubby…. I see it! What is that?

Christopher stands and does not answer and looks down at his shoes. He seems reticent to look at anyone.

| Jennifer (to Christopher and the group): | Christopher, Shane is asking you a question. |
| --- | --- |

Christopher pauses a long time and stares at the wall. It seems like he is trying to avoid Shane's question.

| Shane: | I am expecting an answer. |
| --- | --- |
| Jennifer: | Christopher, answer him! Yes or no? Is that your story in your cubby? |
| Christopher (after a long pause): | That's my old story. I lost my rewrite. |

Five people raise their hands at the same time. Christopher calls on Vince.

| Vince (to Christopher): | Read your old story. |
| --- | --- |

Christopher stands and shakes his head back and forth to indicate "no."

| Jennifer (to Christopher): | You may not shake your head at me. I am talking to you in words. Do you understand me? (Christopher nods.) Yes? OK, then answer me. |
| --- | --- |

Christopher reluctantly pulls out the old story from his cubby and slowly unrolls it. Vince and Christopher talk back and forth.

| Jennifer (to the group): | Does anyone know what is happening here? (She calls on Amber who has raised her hand.) |
| --- | --- |
| Amber (to Christopher): | He (Shane) wants you to go check the paper that McKenzie threw away in the trash and see if it has the same title (as the one Christopher is looking for). |

At this point, Jennifer demands that Christopher stand up and call on people by name to tell him why they have a problem with his doing nothing in writing circle.

Christopher had obviously done no writing that day. Students have high expectations for the writer to be prepared and for the writing itself, but Jennifer has expectations that seem to be unique for each individual student. How she talks to and what she expects from each child is different. There was a challenging tone to writing circle that day and for Christopher the activity was not much fun.

Afterward, the students had a discussion about their feelings and why they were upset with Christopher. They said that they gave him a lot of ideas the day before, and that he did not use any of them (ideas about how to fix the fact that he lost his paper). All the comments they made seemed to indicate that they were upset with him for wasting their time in writing circle.

At times there is a demanding nature to writing circle. The language used and the tone of voice can be quite challenging. I (Frank) remember being concerned in my own room about making the author's chair so much of a "hot seat" that students do not want to sign up for it. The writing circle is intended to support writers in their writing. It seems that we walk a fine line between supporting students and challenging them.

## Assertions Expanded: Student Focus

*Students refer to literature and other classroom "texts" when sharing and talking about their writing.*

This assertion became apparent from looking at the topics, structures, and titles of student writing and the talk that ensued around these pieces. There were striking similarities between formally published pieces—children's picture books, for example—and the students' own writing. Students borrowed ideas constantly and used the texts that were made available to them to support their writing. This concept has been called "intertextuality," and refers to the idea that all texts are understood or interpreted in relation to other experienced texts (Barthes, 1979).

During the writing circle, we noticed that when children were asked where they got their ideas for their stories, they often referred to the authors of the books that were read aloud and discussed in class. Not only were the topics similar, but the language and structure in these stories showed remarkable similarities. For example, students would often begin their stories with the opening, "Once Upon a Time…" or include specific characters like Rainbow Fish, Big Al, and Winnie the Pooh.

The following excerpt illustrates the talk that took place concerning one student's piece of writing. Tiffany, a 7-year-old girl in Rebecca's classroom, had signed up to read her piece of writing titled *The Very Small Lamb*. This was a story about a little lamb that was constantly being pushed around by the flock because of her size. Every time this happened the mother lamb would tell her that she loved her no matter her size. It had a section of the text that was repeated throughout the piece, "No matter how small you are, I'll still love you." The vignette illustrates the student's knowledge of one of the authors discussed in our classroom that she uses to support her style of writing and choice of language.

> Tiffany finishes reading her story in the writing circle. Jessica, another student, asks her what it is that she needs help with today. Tiffany tells the students that she wants some help to add more ideas to her story and that she also wants ideas for an ending. Tiffany then calls on children to listen to their comments.
>
> Emma describes the picture that Tiffany's writing creates in her head. She explains that she loses her picture because Tiffany has not finished the story. She suggests that Tiffany take more time and finish telling the class what happened to the lamb. Tiffany's response is short and to the point as she states, "He walked for awhile and then they went home. That's all I'll tell you for now."

Rebecca interjects and asks Emma to explain what gives her the "picture in her head." Emma explains that it is the words that make her think about the green grass and the hot sun, and she felt sorry for the lamb. Tiffany smiles and nods in agreement. Rebecca turns to Tiffany and asks her how she chose the words to "paint such a picture."

Tiffany explains, "First, I thought of the title. Then I thought of something really nice, and then just thought of nice words."

Rebecca asks what she was thinking about when she was writing these words. She replies, "I was thinking of *Time for Bed* and *Koala Lou*. The repeating parts are from *Koala Lou* and the little lamb part is from *Time for Bed*."

Another child speaks out saying, "It is kind of like *Koala Lou* because of the 'No matter how small you are, I still love you'" [part].

During the weeks preceding this discussion in the writing circle, the class had been doing an author study on the writings of Mem Fox. The children had been involved in choosing the stories to read and developed an admiration for her stories. The children began to attend to specific components of her stories, like the repetition in *Koala Lou* and the illustrations in *Time for Bed*. Different children in the classroom, Tiffany in particular, used various author's styles to support their writing. Tiffany drew from the writings of Mem Fox to support her story, borrowing specific structures and language from the author. This is an example of intertextuality.

The children were exposed to a wide variety of genres throughout the year, and became aware of different elements of each genre. Through class discussions and the creation of charts that listed components of a specific genre, the children were able to identify various types of stories when they were read and discussed. They were able to incorporate these specific elements into their writing. The following dialogue is an example of how the children used their knowledge of genres to incorporate specific elements of writing into their stories.

Emma was writing a story about a prince and princess. Her story began with "Once upon a time…." After reading her piece to the class, the following discussion took place:

Rosa:    Your story sounded like a fairy tale.

Pete:    No because she needs magic and a bad guy. Fairy tales always have magic and bad guys. How about a dragon?

Emma:    I think it should be a person.

Devon:    Add the prince "fighted" the bad guys.

Vern:    Put "the bad guys fight the evil."

Emma:    I'll add that.

Lydia:    The prince can get hurt.

| Emma: | He doesn't have to get hurt. |
|---|---|
| Manuel: | You could put "somebody was trying to get the princess." |
| Devon: | The bad guys were all dead. The prince was mad 'cause he didn't have anybody to fight. |
| Emma: | That doesn't happen. |
| Tiffany: | In a fairy tale there has to be a happy ending. You could put "the prince saves the princess from the bad guys or the dragon." Whatever. |
| Manuel: | What is the King and Queen's name? |
| Emma: | It doesn't matter. But maybe I'll add that. |
| Ed: | The princess should be called Emma and the prince called Larry. |

(Laughter breaks out. Larry is another child in the class.)

| Emma: | OK. I like that. |
|---|---|
| Devon: | Are you going to add an ending? |
| Emma: | When I get there. |
| Kent: | It has to have an ending. All stories have an ending and it should be happy. Most fairy tales have happy endings. If you are writing a fairy tale you have to have a happy ending. |
| Pete: | Could the dragon scorch the princess? |
| Emma: | No. I won't put that. Besides, there is no dragon. It's an evil person. |
| Manuel: | There could be some magic powder. |
| Emma: | I'll think about that. |
| Teacher (Rebecca): | What is your plan? Are you going to use some of these ideas? |
| Emma: | My mouth is zipped. It's a secret. You have to wait until I publish. |

Not only did students refer to specific pieces of literature, but their talk also focused on the specific elements of particular genres. Fairy tales were a genre that had been discussed at length and "charts" were created to contain ideas as they evolved over the course of the discussions. It became obvious that the literature being read in the class had an influence on the students' writing. The structures and style of the writing of various authors supported the efforts of students throughout the writing process.

*Students use talk during the writing circle to create their definitions of what it means to be a writer/author.*

The talk in writing circle often focused on children describing their perspectives about being a writer. The definition of a writer was not given to the students by the teacher, rather it was constructed over the course of the year through the children's talk. Even though there were common threads that ran through the various definitions each child created, each child also had an individual perspective about authorship. It was talk—the actual student discourse—that played a prominent role in developing the student's sense of being a writer.

The first month of school seems to be the appropriate time to talk about "What is a writer?" and "What does a writer do?" However, these questions continue to be revisited throughout the children's journey of creating and sharing stories. Children come to the writing circle with a novice understanding of what it means to be a writer and this understanding becomes more sophisticated as the year progresses. Through the talk during the writer's circle, the students redefined their understandings of what it means to be a writer and what writers do. The following transcript is used to illustrate this assertion.

| | |
|---|---|
| Katy (stands up): | I need more ideas. (It is Katy's turn today to read her story aloud to the class. She begins by calling on students with their hands raised for comments and ideas.) |
| Jed: | There's a lot of details! [referring to her story] |
| Katy: | What are details? |
| Jed: | They tell a lot and make you a good person. |
| Teacher (Jennifer) (interrupting): | A good person or a good writer? |
| Jed: | A good writer. |
| Teacher: | So what does it [a good writer] look like? |
| Jed: | They write good because…(pauses) it's like if somebody…(wrinkles forehead and stops). |
| Teacher: | How do you learn to write? |
| Class (in unison): | By a teacher. |
| Jed: | By someone who's already written. |
| Zane: | By your mind. Like your brain's figuring it out, you can look at the alphabet to figure out the letter of the sound. |
| Shane: | What if you're writing a word and you don't know what comes next? |
| Rachel: | Maybe you can… |
| Shane: | You can learn it out of a book. |

| Jed: | Like Shakespeare! |
|------|-------------------|
| Shane: | Well I was thinking about the book Jennifer (teacher) read yesterday, *Amber on the Mountain.* |
| Jed: | But that one had a lot of experienced writers. Young writers have to think more than old writers because they've [old writers] done it so long. |
| Shane: | They're professionals. |
| Teacher: | So how do you get to be a professional writer? |
| Jed: | You have to practice and practice and practice. |
| Shane: | Until you know every letter in every word or copy it out of a book. |
| Tony: | Or by just sounding it out. |
| Teacher: | Do we always know every word or copy it? |
| Shane: | No, I was just thinking of…you know the blue book we use? (points to large blue dictionary on the library bookshelves) |
| Rachel: | The dictionary? |
| Shane: | Yeah. |

The discussion then faded and Jennifer asked, "Would it help us when we get stuck if we had a chart of What a Writer Does?" The class agreed that they should write their ideas and display the chart on the classroom wall. The following items were listed on the chart that day:

What a Writer Does

- Sounds out words
- Uses the alphabet
- Uses the dictionary
- Asks friends
- Uses other books/stories
- Uses the library and student "research"
- Gets ideas from things you know a lot about

As shown in this example, there were many times when the student talk would take a direction other than the one intended by the student author. It was during these "detours" that the group was able to share its opinions and ideas from personal or shared experiences of what a writer does. In this sense, talk was used to share and develop understanding about the nature of writing and being a writer. Jennifer noticed that the students often focused on an element of writing; in this example it was Jed's idea of detail that led the class to a deeper discussion of writing. Although the teacher interjected and posed the question "What does a good writer look like," the students were in charge of constructing their definition through talk. At the beginning of the year, the children were prepared with a commonly heard answer concerning how you learn to write. They would answer, "A teacher." Through these discussions students came to realize that not only did teachers support students as writers, but the students themselves supported and affected each other's definition of what it means to be a writer. As the year progressed, the children referred to themselves more as writers, however, references to "becoming a writer" or "professional writer" continued to come up in their discussions.

*Students viewed the writing circle as an oral reading event as well as a writing event.*
Our focus on the writing circle as primarily a writing event shifted during the interviews conducted with our students. The students referred again and again to their concerns about reading their writing pieces aloud. They discussed their preparations for their upcoming turn in the writing circle when they would get to read their pieces of writing aloud. Although we focused on the writing circle as primarily a writing event, the children also viewed the writing circle as an oral reading event, often preparing at length for their presentations. Students would gather together to offer each other advice about reading aloud and give each other suggestions during the actual reading. It became obvious that reading their stories aloud with confidence and fluency was an important expectation of the group during the writing circle.

In order to get a better understanding of what the children perceived as the function of the writing circle, we held a discussion during one particular writing circle in which Frank asked Jennifer's class questions about their role in the writing circle.

Frank began with the question, "Why do you sign up for writing circle?" The responses varied from issues about the specific content of the piece of writing to the procedures of the writing process. Though the interview contained responses that referred to other items, the following refer to the assertion that the writing circle is also a reading "event." One student replied, "It [reading to the class] helps you to read your story better, keep on reading," while another said, "Everyone helps you to learn to read and write."

Another question Frank asked was, "What does it feel like when you are the writer who is sharing?" One child responded, "I get nervous when I read," and another said, "Nervous, there are a lot of people when you are reading, they are watching you." Still another replied, "Nervous, when people can't hear me and they tell me to speak louder." We found that many of the responses related to the reading aloud of the piece, not the piece of writing being shared.

This interview revealed a perspective that we had not focused on, namely, the writing circle as an oral reading event. The focus of our project had been the student talk about writing during the writer's circle, but this interview along with student comments made during the daily classroom discussions such as, "You need to practice reading before you come to the circle again" or "You need to use a playground voice when you read so we can understand what you are saying," broadened our understanding of the student's perspective concerning the writing circle.

Students were expected to read fluently if they were sharing their stories during the writing circle. The class seemed almost unwilling to help with the piece of writing if the author could not read it well enough to be understood. Some students would spend an entire week practicing reading their story in order to prepare for sharing during the writer's circle. These observations forced us to consider the implications of the writing circle being an oral performance as much as a writing event.

*Student talk demonstrates noticeable differences between the type of talk concerning the actual content of the story, and the talk that focused on the mechanics of the story.*

During the writing circle, the talk concerning a child's piece of writing would usually focus on either the content of the story or how the story was written. In the beginning of the year, students would often ask for ideas about what else to include in their stories. As the year progressed, the focus of the talk shifted from the content of the story to the mechanics of the story, when students perceived a discrepancy between what the child wanted to say and how it was written or told. The discussions shifted between the content and the mechanics depending on the person sharing the piece of writing, the writer's level of expertise, and the group's expectations for that writer.

The following example illustrates how the grammatical errors in a piece of writing kept the students from being able to focus on the content of the story during the discussion in the writing circle. The discussion never got to what Larry asked from the group because students were focused on the grammatical inconsistencies apparent to them in his piece of writing.

Larry read a story titled *Our Class*, about what people in the classroom do when they are at school. Before Larry read the story, one student asked, "What are we listening for?" We continue with the transcript at the point where Larry is answering that student's question.

| Larry (responding to the student's question): | An ending. (Larry reads his story.) |
|---|---|
| Jack: | What are you reading? |
| Larry: | *Our School.* I need an ending! |
| Tiffany: | How about "School is where I like to be." |
| Larry: | That's closer. |

| | |
|---|---|
| Ed: | "I like school." |
| Larry: | (nods and smiles) |
| Kent: | You said….Read that first part again. |
| Larry (rereads from his story): | "Kyle go to lunch." |
| Kent: | That doesn't sound right. It should be "He GOES to lunch, not he GO." It's the same for "Mrs. Willey GOES to lunch." |
| Larry: | I get it. |
| Manuel: | When you said, "Manuel go to the playground" it doesn't make sense. |
| Emma: | It should be "Manuel GOES to the playground." |
| Larry: | OK. I'll fix it! |
| Teacher (Rebecca): | It sounds like you need to fix some things before we can help you with your ending. Let's talk about something for a moment. (Larry sits down, somewhat frustrated.) |

Larry grew frustrated with the discussion after he realized his mistake concerning verb usage. As obvious from the transcript, he never received the help he asked for. The class could not help with his ending because they were hung up on the grammatical inconsistencies in his piece of writing. Rebecca allowed the discussion to proceed hoping that it would provide an opportunity to demonstrate the proper grammatical structure for his piece.

Following the discussion during the writing circle mentioned above, Rebecca took the opportunity to teach a minilesson to the entire class about the use of verbs in a story. She also discussed how to make a story sound like it happened in the past, present, or future by changing verb tense. This was not a planned lesson. It came about as a response to the interactions that occurred in the writing circle.

## Final Thoughts

The writing circle offers both students and teachers the opportunity to interact with each other about their writing, support each other as writers, and receive feedback for their efforts. The writing circle is also an opportunity for teachers to listen to the voices of the student writers in their class, and use the information gained through listening and careful observations to teach the elements and craft of writing, procedures for the writing workshop, and how to successfully interact within the writing circle itself. The teaching that occurs in the writing circle occurs in an authentic social context that is supported by the interactions between students and teachers.

Though students did not refer to "talk" using that term, talk became synonymous with sharing. For the students, talking became the primary vehicle for sharing and responding to a classmate's writing. Talk was the medium of teaching and learning, and it changed as the context and the participants changed.

Just as reading and writing are now seen by us as inseparable, talking is the third component involved in this interaction. Reading and writing are not silent events. Talk is the medium we use to share our ideas, concerns, and expectations about our development as literate human beings.

We (the teachers) became better listeners as we focused on the interactions during our writing circle. We also came to know our children better and felt more confident in our abilities to support their writing. We worked hard to create a safe and supportive environment where children could grow as writers, yet we still maintained high expectations for our students, challenging them at times to try harder and accept more responsibility for their learning.

We realized our original perspective and purposes for the writing circle had changed. We came to understand that the children needed to be intimately involved in the decisions made about the writing workshop, as we created space for their talk and their writing. The students in our classes held high expectations for themselves as writers, and these expectations were shared in the writing circle. We came to understand that there is more to these interactions than the sharing of pieces of writing. Students shared their lives, their experiences, and their understandings while they created a vision of what it means to be a writer.

## References

Atwell, N. (1998). *In the middle: New understandings about writing, reading, and learning.* Portsmouth, NH: Heinemann.

Barthes, R. (1979). *The pleasure of the text* (R. Miller, Trans.). New York: Hill and Wang.

Calkins, L.M. (1994). *The art of teaching writing.* Portsmouth, NH: Heinemann.

Edelsky, C., Altwerger, B., & Flores, B. (1991). *Whole language: What's the difference?* Portsmouth, NH: Heinemann.

Graves, D. (1983). *Writing: Teachers and children at work.* Portsmouth, NH: Heinemann.

Harste, J., Short, K., & Burke, C. (1988). *Creating classrooms for authors.* Portsmouth, NH: Heinemann.

Jaeger, E.L. (1996). The reading specialist as collaborative consultant. *The Reading Teacher, 49,* 622–629.

Vygotsky, L.S. (1978). *Mind in society: The development of higher psychological processes.* (M. Cole, V.J. Steiner, S. Scribner, & E. Souberman, Eds. & Trans.). Boston: Harvard University Press. (Original work published 1934)

# Beyond the Words on the Page: The Reading Conference as a Forum for Language Development

*George Hunt and Brian Richards*

Much has been made of both the similarities and differences in linguistic interaction at home and at school. Using data from the Bristol Study of Language Development, Wells (1981, 1986) and MacLure and French (1981) showed that although children starting school have already become familiar with the types of interactional structure they will encounter there, there are disparities between the two contexts in the frequency of opportunities for engaging in certain types of conversation. At school, children may not demonstrate the true extent of their communicative abilities. For example, at school they have fewer conversational turns, make fewer requests, and are less likely to ask questions, initiate interactions with adults, or have their own contributions extended. They express a narrower range of meanings, using language that is grammatically less complex than the language they use at home. Similar findings are reported by Tizard and Hughes (1984)—children, in this case girls, engaged in richer conversations at home than at school. At least in part, this difference is the result of the demands of a multichild context in which managing and directing activities and behavior take priority (Wells, 1986). The picture that emerges is of a relatively passive role for the child in typically responding to a predominance of Initiation-Response-Feedback sequences (Hughes & Westgate, 1997; Westgate & Hughes, 1997), and of an asymmetry of rights (MacLure & French, 1981) between children and teachers to choose topics, initiate interactional sequences, influence turn-taking, and explore their own meanings. In short, children have little access to the agenda (Richards, 1990), that is to say, they have little control over the subject matter and direction of the discussion.

However, one might expect the reading conference to redress the balance and afford a richer context for the development and exploration of language. After all, in addition to its contribution to emerging literacy, the reading con-

ference presents the opportunity for one-to-one interaction with a linguistically mature adult in a situation that can incorporate many of the features thought
to facilitate language development (see Gallaway & Richards, 1994; Ninio &
Bruner, 1978; Richards & Gallaway, 1999; Snow & Goldfield, 1983; Wells, 1986).
These include the joint focus of attention on, and joint engagement with, the
message of the text. In this dyadic or paired situation the child will have more
opportunity to contribute, take initiative, ask questions, and initiate conversational sequences. This makes possible a more responsive style on the part of
the adult typified by a higher frequency of semantically contingent adult responses such as expansions, recasts, and semantic extensions or "move-ons."
What these teacher actions have in common is that their starting point is what
the child has just said. Extensions or "move-ons" extend the child's meaning and
topic, and provide scaffolding for further contributions to the conversation.
Recasts and expansions repeat the child's meaning in an upgraded or alternative
form in which vocabulary, syntax, or morphology is enriched. Such responses
offer implicit feedback without criticism because they are a natural part of conversational exchanges, but they nevertheless pass on lexical and structural information that children can include in their own utterances through processes
of repetition and imitation (Speidel & Nelson, 1989).

In the United Kingdom, and particularly since the introduction of a statu-
tory National Curriculum in 1989, it has become common practice for tasks
such as reading with children to be shared with, or even delegated to, trained
or untrained assistants and voluntary helpers, often parents. Such classroom assistants are now available in most primary (elementary) schools, particularly in
the younger grades. In theory, the availability of such assistance ought to increase the frequency of children's contributions to dyadic or, at least, small-
group conversations. In addition, the existence of different adult conversational
partners in the classroom should provide a range of conversational experiences varying in the degree to which they provide fine-tuning and scaffolding.
These could be seen as providing a "bridge" or a series of "bridges" between the
child-friendly world of shared, implicitly understood meanings of the home,
and the more rigorous communicative demands of the outside, where the lack
of preexisting mutual understanding and knowledge requires greater explicitness
and decontextualization.

The "bridge hypothesis" was first formulated by Berko Gleason (1975) in response to the observation that the discourse of fathers appeared to accommodate less to the immature language of their children than that of mothers.
Comparisons between mothers and fathers interacting with the same child
showed that although fathers made many of the speech adjustments typical of
the "motherese" register (Newport, 1977) such as prosodic modification, shorter
and less complex utterances, and limited vocabulary, their lower level of familiarity with the child, his or her activities, knowledge, and (at times idiosyncrat-

ic) language resulted in less responsiveness to children's utterances, a more directive style, and a greater likelihood of conversational breakdown (Barton & Tomasello, 1994). As a consequence, children who experience regular interaction with both a primary and secondary caregiver are likely to be faced with two contrasting styles of conversation. The first, with the primary caregiver (regardless of gender), may be highly supportive and accommodative, a rich context for the acquisition of language—phonology, grammar, and vocabulary. Interaction with the secondary caregiver requires children to adapt to their conversation partners and can be seen more as a forum for pragmatic development—the development of the conversational skills required to put acquired linguistic knowledge into action with a less accommodating partner.

If the secondary caregiver can be seen as a bridge for developing the communication skills required in the outside community, then it is possible to conceptualize conversational experience with a variety of interlocutors (or conversational partners) as a series of bridges depending on the degree of accommodation they provide for the child. Mannle and Tomasello (1987) for example have extended the notion of the "father bridge" to the "sibling bridge" (pp. 36–37). In the same way, it may be possible to discern graded levels of discourse accommodation in interactions with different adults during the reading conference that correlate with dimensions such as their training, experience, or familiarity with the child. It is to investigate this hypothesis and to evaluate the reading conference as a setting to facilitate the development of language and communication that the study to be described in this chapter was designed.

## The Reading Conference

As noted, the reading conference would seem to provide a promising environment for language development. Typically, these occasions are centered on oral reading with a teacher or another adult listening to the child and providing help of various kinds in the decoding and comprehension of a book. This help might include direct teaching of graphophonic relationships, references to how the content of the text relates to the child's real-life experiences, and drawing attention to book illustrations. In the more interactive type of conference advocated by, for example, Arnold (1982) and Waterland (1985), support also might take the form of reading to or with the child, eliciting the child's opinions about the book, and encouraging the child to raise his or her own questions. Here there would be a joint focus of attention, shared purpose, and many opportunities for open-ended conversation about topics that are of interest to the child.

Benefits to language development might also arise from the fact that the use of classroom assistants referred to earlier should mean that the range of interlocutors is not confined to adults with a narrow instructional agenda. It could be hypothesized that parent volunteer interlocutors would be in a better position than teachers to offer rich conversation to children for the following reasons:

- Children's relationships with assistants are likely to be less formal than their relationships with teachers.
- Assistants are not under the same time and attention constraints as teachers, who, while attending to an individual reader, maintain responsibility for the rest of the class.
- As members of the local community, assistants are likely to be more familiar with the child's extramural social life, and hence be in a better position to make links between the text and the child's experiences.

In light of the literature referred to earlier, in order for reading conversations to fulfill their potential to facilitate language development, we would expect to find the following characteristics:

- Evidence of symmetrical conversational rights: The child contributing to the course of the conversation by, for example, asking questions based on the text, or making links between the text and aspects of his or her life.
- Adult responses to child contributions that extend topics initiated by the child.
- Adult initiations and responses that encourage the child to talk by inviting the child to link text meaning to experience.

The study described here investigates whether or not the potential of reading conferences for language development is being realized in the context of one educational setting. It attempts to answer three principal questions. First, to what extent does the reading conference offer conversational symmetry? Second, to what extent does the reading conference encourage the child to talk about links between reading and everyday experience? Last, are there any differences in these respects between the conversational styles of teachers and those of parent and other classroom assistants?

## Method of Research

Audio recordings were made of reading conferences in an infant school in Berkshire, United Kingdom. The adult participants were five teachers and the five parent volunteer assistants who worked with them. The parent volunteers were not related to the child participants. Each member of the teacher-assistant partnership was recorded in a reading conversation with the same target child from the teacher's class, the tape recordings of teacher-child interactions being made on a different day from those of parent-child interactions. The children were in reception (kindergarten), or mixed reception and year one classes and were between 5 and 6 years old. All were classified by their teachers as being nonreaders or in the very early stages of learning to read. The conversations varied in length from just over 2 minutes to just over 12 minutes and the circumstances in which the recordings were made reflected normal classroom practice. Audio recording, rather than video recording, was used because of difficulties in obtaining teachers' cooperation for the latter.

The conversations were transcribed using the Codes for the Human Analysis of Transcripts (CHAT) format of the Child Language Data Exchange System (CHILDES) (MacWhinney, 1995; MacWhinney & Snow, 1990) and analyzed qualitatively and quantitatively. The associated Computerized Language Analysis (CLAN) programs were then used to create vocabulary lists for each participant and to compute word type and word token totals, mean length of utterance (MLU), and mean length of turn (MLT) (see Table 1). Utterances were classified into initiation, response, and feedback moves (Sinclair & Coulthard, 1975), and initiations were further coded according to the way in which they were intended to direct the interlocutor's attention. The following categories were suggested by the qualitative analysis of the transcripts.

Initiations that make links between text meaning and real-life experience:

*Child: My friend's got that cat.*

*(Child points to a picture in the book)*

Initiations that focus attention on word recognition, including prompts to identify whole words and to sound out letters:

*Adult: What's the first sound in that word?*

Initiations that focus on aspects of the book other than meaning or word recognition:

*Adult: Right Jane, what kind of book is this?*

Initiations that direct the behavior of the interlocutor:

*Adult: Want to sit closer?*

Each adult participant also completed a brief questionnaire (see Figure 1) about their beliefs concerning the role of the adult in helping children to read. This consisted of six statements with a 5-point Likert scale, and three open-ended questions. The statements had been derived from earlier interviews with parents and teachers and were concerned with the value of talking about the pictures or story, guessing unknown words, sounding out letters, keeping attention focused on the pages, and whether poor reading ability was attributable to laziness.

**TABLE 1**
**Quantitative measures of contribution to the conversation**

| | Duration (minutes:seconds) | Word tokens | Word types | Utterances | MLU | MLT |
|---|---|---|---|---|---|---|
| Child 1 | 10:35 | 371 | 131 | 107 | 3.4 | 4.0 |
| Parent 1 | | 661 | 182 | 153 | 4.3 | 7.1 |
| Child 1 | 08:40 | 229 | 125 | 90 | 2.6 | 3.1 |
| Teacher 1 | | 618 | 227 | 128 | 4.6 | 7.6 |
| Child 2 | 02:17 | 105 | 32 | 23 | 3.5 | 4.2 |
| Parent 2 | | 80 | 43 | 33 | 3.2 | 5.2 |
| Child 2 | 09:21 | 391 | 105 | 91 | 4.4 | 5.3 |
| Teacher 2 | | 543 | 181 | 134 | 4.1 | 7.2 |
| Child 3 | 04:30 | 60 | 34 | 33 | 2.0 | 2.1 |
| Parent 3 | | 561 | 188 | 107 | 5.3 | 17.0 |
| Child 3 | 07:00 | 83 | 34 | 49 | 1.7 | 1.9 |
| Teacher 3 | | 562 | 166 | 132 | 4.3 | 12.2 |
| Child 4 | 04:10 | 170 | 55 | 53 | 3.2 | 4.0 |
| Parent 4 | | 290 | 106 | 73 | 4.0 | 6.7 |
| Child 4 | 12:18 | 448 | 127 | 136 | 3.3 | 3.9 |
| Teacher 4 | | 1329 | 302 | 249 | 5.4 | 11.4 |
| Child 5 | 02:55 | 125 | 52 | 34 | 3.7 | 4.5 |
| Parent 5 | | 282 | 119 | 52 | 5.4 | 9.7 |
| Child 5 | 06:05 | 175 | 92 | 64 | 2.7 | 3.0 |
| Teacher 5 | | 456 | 150 | 115 | 4.0 | 7.9 |

*Note*: MLU = mean length of utterance (in words). MLT = mean length of turn (in words).

# Results of the Study

## The Questionnaire

The questionnaire responses revealed a clear consensus that the reading conference should be a relaxed, enjoyable, social event for both parties. The statements advocating discussion of pictures, stories, and guesswork while reading were scored consistently higher than those that favored sounding out letters, close attention to the page, or the attribution of reading difficulties to laziness.

---

**FIGURE 1**
**Questionnaire and responses**

---

Open-ended questions
1. How do you think reading aloud with an adult helps a child to read alone?
2. Apart from learning about reading, are there any other ways in which sharing books with an adult is good for a child?
3. What would you say is the best way of helping a child to read?

Statements
1. Children should be encouraged to talk about pictures when reading.
2. Talking to children about stories is as important as getting them to read the words on the page.
3. Getting children to guess unknown words is a good way of helping them to learn to read.
4. Sounding out letters is the most important way of reading unknown words.
5. Some children have difficulties in reading because they are lazy.
6. Children should be encouraged to keep their attention on the page when they are reading.

Responses to six statements above
(1: Strongly disagree—5: Strongly agree)

|    | T1 | P1 | T2 | P2 | T3 | P3 | T4 | P4 | T5 | P5 |
|----|----|----|----|----|----|----|----|----|----|----|
| 1. | 5 | 5 | 3 | 5 | 3 | 3 | 5 | 5 | 5 | 5 |
| 2. | 5 | 4 | 3 | 5 | 5 | 4 | 5 | 5 | 5 | 5 |
| 3. | 5 | 3 | 3 | 5 | 5 | 5 | 5 | 5 | 5 | 3 |
| 4. | 5* | 4 | 4 | 5 | 5* | 3 | 4 | 2 | 4* | 5 |
| 5. | 1 | 2 | 2 | 3 | 1 | 1 | 1 | 4 | 1 | 3 |
| 6. | 5 | 4 | 3 | 5 | 5 | 4 | 3 | 4 | 4 | 4 |

\* Respondents added a rider to the effect that phonic decoding was *one* important strategy for reading.
T = teacher respondent, P = parent respondent

---

In their open-ended responses, both parents and teachers stressed the importance of modeling enthusiasm for reading, building confidence by providing encouragement, and developing relationships through discussion. The responses suggest a belief in both the affective and the cognitive benefits of promoting conversation during the reading conference. Typical responses from teachers include the following:

*"An adult will give the child confidence through positive feedback."*

*"Discussing the content—developing vocabulary and story patterns."*

*"Sharing ideas and thoughts about the story/facts and extending ideas."*

*"Lots of talk about shared experience."*

Typical parent responses include:

> *"Being relaxed, smiling, and positive—a happy experience for adult and child."*
>
> *"Develop discussion about the story using pictures."*
>
> *"Fun activities—reading almost accidentally."*
>
> *"It is a time of closeness for both adult and child to develop personal relationships."*

Only one response, from a parent, deviated from this pattern:

> *"I sometimes feel that reading with an adult is onerous for the child; maybe he/she does not focus on the text."*

## *Analysis of the Transcripts*

Interestingly, both qualitative and quantitative analysis of the transcripts revealed that the beliefs in the value of conversation expressed in the questionnaires were not being realized in practice. All the conversations displayed extreme asymmetry of participation. As can be seen in Table 1, the indicators of quantity of participation in conversation are consistently and substantially in favor of the adult. There are only three exceptions to this pattern in the whole table. Furthermore, there was no difference between the teachers and the parents. This can be seen for selected measures in Table 2.

In fact, further analysis showed that both categories of adult assumed almost complete control over the content of the conversations. With the exception of one conversation, children's contributions were almost entirely confined to making responses to adult initiations. As can be seen from Table 3, child initiations were very rare. On average they made up only 13.5% of the 497 initiations identified in the total sample. Analysis of the adult initiations showed they were largely focused on directing children's attention to lexical and sub-

**TABLE 2**
**Comparison of mean child contribution with parents and teachers**

| | Interlocutor | |
| --- | --- | --- |
| Measure of child participation | Parent | Teacher |
| Mean MLU | 3.2 | 2.9 |
| Mean MLT | 3.8 | 3.4 |
| Mean % total utterances | 37.5 | 35.9 |
| Mean % total initiations | 11.9 | 10.8 |

lexical features of text through direct questions and intonational prompts (see excerpts). This is reflected in Table 3 in the low proportion of adult initiations that make text to life or life to text links. Although all adults did make at least one text to life or life to text link in the course of the conference, such links amounted in total to only 15.6% of the 430 adult initiations in the sample. By contrast, when child initiations were made, they took the form of utterances that linked text to life or life to text in at least 50% of instances and in some cases (Children 2 and 3) in 100% of instances.

Adult responses to children's text to life and life to text initiations, and the feedback they provided for children's responses to their own such initiations, did show a degree of contingency. That is, they did respond to the child's meaning and build on it. However, they also tended to be cursory in comparison with the perseverant nature of text-focusing initiations and feedback to children's text-based responses. Children's initiations were always acknowledged and positively responded to, but they were never allowed to divert attention from the graphophonic dimension for more than two or three turns of the conversation. This can be illustrated by the following example of a child initiating a text to life link, followed by an adult response and a refocusing move directing the child's attention to the lexical and sublexical aspects of the text.

## TABLE 3
## Proportion of child versus adult initiations and life to text or text to life links

|  | Total initiations | Child | | Adult | |
|---|---|---|---|---|---|
|  |  | % of total | % T<>L | % of total | % T<>L |
| Ch – parent 1 | 74 | 41.9 | 54.8 | 58.1 | 23.2 |
| Ch – teacher 1 | 61 | 22.9 | 100.0 | 77.1 | 27.6 |
| Ch – parent 2 | 15 | 0 | – | 100.0 | 13.3 |
| Ch – teacher 2 | 63 | 14.5 | 50.0 | 85.5 | 3.6 |
| Ch – parent 3 | 30 | 0 | – | 100.0 | 6.6 |
| Ch – teacher 3 | 63 | 0 | – | 100.0 | 11.1 |
| Ch – parent 4 | 27 | 3.8 | 100.0 | 96.2 | 19.2 |
| Ch – teacher 4 | 74 | 7.7 | 100.0 | 92.3 | 13.0 |
| Ch – parent 5 | 29 | 13.8 | 75.0 | 86.2 | 48.0 |
| Ch – teacher 5 | 61 | 6.5 | 50.0 | 93.5 | 8.8 |

T<>L: text to life or life to text

(The child has been looking at a picture of a bird embryo in the egg and the teacher has compared it with a human embryo.)

| | |
|---|---|
| Child: | Does it start off with just the head? |
| Adult: | A human baby? |
| Child: | Yes. |
| Adult: | It starts off as a tiny little cell, and then it gets bigger. |
| Adult: | I'm not sure whether the head comes first or the all parts gradually develop. |
| Adult: | (refocusing on text) "All…" |
| Child: | (reading) "All birds have babies." |
| Adult: | No look it doesn't begin with *buh* does it? |
| Child: | *fff.* |
| Adult: | So what is it all birds have? |
| Child: | (indistinct) |
| Adult: | *fff.* |
| Child: | Food. |
| Adult: | No. |
| Adult: | We talked about this. |
| Adult: | All birds have…? |
| Child: | Wings. |
| Adult: | That doesn't begin with *fuh*. |
| Adult: | What do all birds have that begins with *fuh*? |
| Child: | Feathers. |
| Adult: | Yes. |

Much of the range of vocabulary in the children's contributions was accounted for by recitation of the text rather than spontaneous usage. The adults' preoccupation with a word by word replication of the text resulted in there being very little spontaneous language in the contributions made by the children. Many of their utterances consisted of single words, phonemes, or phoneme clusters. The following transaction, in which a teacher attempts to help the child identify the word *with*, occupied almost 2 minutes of a 12-minute session. During the transaction the child makes only two utterances longer than a word. Both are two-word text replication attempts, and both are truncated by the teacher's corrective feedback.

| | |
|---|---|
| Adult: | What's that first sound there? |
| Adult: | Can you read…? |
| Child: | *Wuh.* |
| Adult: | Yes. |
| Child: | *Ih tuh huh.* |
| Adult: | Ah, you've got your sounds right. |
| Adult: | What happens when those two little sounds go together, when those letters go together? |
| Child: | Had. |
| Adult: | Let's have a look there. |
| Adult: | (reads) Sam said let's play…? |
| Adult: | Try the sounds together there. |
| Child: | Its. |
| Adult: | No look, but you were right the first time with it. |
| Child: | *Wuh ih tuh wit.* |
| Adult: | No just the little bit I'm showing you there. |
| Child: | *Wuh ih.* |
| Adult: | Put those together and what have you got? |
| Child: | *Wuh ih tuh wit.* |
| Adult: | What little sound does that make? |
| Adult: | No can you see what I'm showing you there? |
| Child: | *Wuh ih.* |
| Adult: | No, now what does that say? |
| Adult: | Those two little letters put those together. |
| Child: | *Uh.* |
| Adult: | *With.* |
| Child: | *Wit.* |
| Adult: | That's it *with* yes. |
| Child: | *With.* |
| Adult: | Let's read it. |
| Adult: | Sam said let's play…? |
| Child: | Let's play *wih…weh…* |
| Adult: | Those two sounds…? |

| Child: | Have. |
|--------|-------|
| Adult: | Let's have a little look again. |
| Adult: | Those two words letters there. |
| Child: | Sam makes… |
| Adult: | No have a look there. |
| Adult: | Can you see? |
| Child: | Had. |
| Adult: | No, no, don't guess. |
| Adult: | Have a little look now. |
| Adult: | We've got those two letters there. |
| Adult: | We put them together and they make a different sound. |
| Adult: | I wonder if you can remember? |
| Child: | *Uh.* |
| Adult: | A *t* and an *h* together make a…? |
| Child: | *Thuh.* |
| Adult: | Good boy. |
| Adult: | Let's put our sounds together now. |
| Adult: | Sam said let's play *wuh?* |
| Child: | *With.* |
| Adult: | Good boy. |

## Analysis and Discussion

This study addressed three main areas: The extent to which the reading conference offers conversational symmetry, how far the child is encouraged to talk about links between reading and everyday experience, and whether the conversational styles of teachers and parent volunteers provide qualitatively different conversational experiences. In summary, it was found that, notwithstanding questionnaire responses that expressed commitment to flexible and wide-ranging talk about books, both parents and teachers dominated the reading conference and confined children's responses to a large extent to decoding the text. In fact, all the adults in this study said they valued the practice of engaging children in conversation with a book as a joint focus of attention. However, there is clearly a tension between the idealized vision of the reading conference depicted in questionnaire responses and the way in which adults talk with children when they are learning to read in school.

The findings recorded here illustrate the dilemma faced by early years teachers and their assistants, who are responsible for developing both spoken language and literacy. Facilitating the child's participation in conversation through a conversation-eliciting style is likely to be of benefit to the process of language development, and a conversation-eliciting style is characterized by low constraint questions, contingency to children's contributions, and a commitment to relative equality of participation (McDonald & Pien, 1982). However, the task of teaching children to read, although potentially a very fertile source of child-initiated conversation, also requires the adult to exercise control over the focus of the child's attention, the material that is read, and the duration of the reading event. The degree of this control is affected by beliefs about the general role of the teacher in classroom interactions, beliefs about the way in which reading should be taught, and the pressures of the curriculum.

Cultural models of classroom discourse and literacy teaching act as powerful constraints on the behavior of all participants in literacy events (Heath, 1983). Parents and other volunteers working in classrooms appear to adapt stereotypical discourse practices, abandoning the diverse voices that might enrich classroom talk (Westgate & Hughes, 1997). All the conversations conformed closely to the adult-initiation, pupil-response, adult-feedback pattern, long established as being typical of classroom interaction (Stubbs, 1975). This pattern creates a pseudodialogue in which the adult's conversational moves are much longer and more complex than the child's, and serve to limit the child's moves to brief responses to convergent questions. The contingencies of everyday conversation, in which content is negotiated in a less determined way by interlocutors of more equal status, are excluded. If one of the aims of classroom conversation is to help children to speak in more extended, complex, and varied ways, then the Initiation-Response-Feedback pattern is an inappropriate one, and its domination of the reading conference will prevent adults and children from actually talking about books in the predictable but flexible routine interactions that have been shown to support progress in language development (Snow & Goldfield, 1983).

Turning to underlying beliefs about literacy teaching, the data suggest that talking about books is not, in practice, the main purpose of the reading conference. All the adult participants appeared to envision the word-by-word replication of the text, through phoneme by phoneme sounding out, as being the primary goal of the conference. Attention to pictures, overall meaning, and relevance of the text to the reader's life were called on mainly as supports to the process of graphophonic replication. Children's attempts to introduce other literacy practices—such as reciting from memory, approximating through guesswork, and talking around the gist of the text—were tacitly or expressly discouraged. It could be posited that the beliefs thus inculcated in children concerning what is expected of them during the reading conference could cause them to ignore or devalue adult attempts to initiate less structured conversation around the text.

Another concern is the nature of the assessment procedures that operate during the reading conference. The interaction between adult and child is valued not just as an opportunity to practice reading skills, but to monitor and record how well these skills are developing. The reading conference has great potential for providing information about the child's ability to use a range of cues in reading, about how well the child is comprehending the text, and about the range of reading the child is experiencing (Barrs & Thomas, 1991). Questionnaire responses indicated that the adults in the study were sensitive to these holistic aspects of reading, but if the attention of both adult and child is largely confined to sublexical aspects of the text, then the opportunity to assess these aspects is not being realized.

These issues have implications for policy and practice. Although teachers and their assistants are under pressure to achieve strictly defined curricular goals, opportunities for providing the relaxed contexts necessary for contingency-rich conversations to take place are not likely to flourish. In the United Kingdom and elsewhere, there is currently a strong political move toward dictated curricula with highly prescriptive objectives. The National Literacy Strategy in England, for example, has recently increased pressure on schools to focus on lexical and sublexical aspects of texts, and to inculcate "a sense of urgency" in teaching (DFEE, 1998, p. 8). One of the National Literacy Strategy's explicit aims is to reduce diversity of practice, and in pursuance of this moves are being made to ensure that classroom helpers use the same strategies as teachers when talking to children about reading. There is a danger here that opportunities for children to hear a variety of voices and conversational styles will be reduced still further.

## Conclusion

The findings outlined here are based on a small sample of children and adults, but both informal observation and anecdotal evidence from similar contexts suggest that the pattern of interaction recorded here could be typical of many early years classrooms. Further research with a larger sample from a range of schools would be needed to confirm this. A more detailed analysis of data and more extensive interviewing of both adult and child participants also would be informative. The current data were collected in the term before the implementation of the UK National Literacy Strategy, so the effects of this initiative on classroom discourse need to be investigated.

One effect that has been immediately apparent under the National Literacy Strategy is the shift from one-to-one reading conferences toward whole-class teaching of word-level work within a designated literacy hour. In spite of this, many schools have made efforts to retain the reading conference because of their beliefs about the value of this experience for children's reading development. There may be a case for retaining the reading conference, possibly confining instructional concerns to the literacy hour, and reestablishing the importance of the reading conference as a time to talk rather than to teach. But given the striking mismatch we have observed between theory and practice, it is important that the reading conference's objectives are clearly defined and appropriate for the age of the child, and its implementation is closely monitored and evaluated by practitioners so that its intended purpose is genuinely achieved.

## References

Arnold, H. (1982). *Listening to children reading.* London: Hodder and Stoughton.

Barrs, M., & Thomas, A. (1991). *The reading book.* London: Centre for Language in Primary Education.

Barton, M.E., & Tomasello, M. (1994). The rest of the family: The role of fathers and siblings in early language development. In C. Gallaway & B.J. Richards (Eds.), *Input and interaction in language acquisition* (pp. 109–134). Cambridge, UK: Cambridge University Press.

Berko Gleason, J. (1975). Fathers and other strangers: Men's speech to young children. *Georgetown Roundtable on Language and Linguistics.* Washington, DC: Georgetown University Press.

Department for Education and Employment. (1998). *The National Literacy Strategy.* London: Department for Education and Employment.

Gallaway, C., & Richards, B.J. (Eds.). (1994). *Input and interaction in language acquisition.* Cambridge, UK: Cambridge University Press.

Heath, S.B. (1983). *Ways with words: Language, life and work in communities and classrooms.* Cambridge, UK: Cambridge University Press.

Hughes, M., & Westgate, D. (1997). Assistants as talk-partners in early-years classrooms: Some issues of support and development. *Educational Review, 49,* 5–12.

McDonald, L., & Pien, D. (1982). Mother conversational behaviour as a function of interactional intent. *Journal of Child Language, 9,* 337–358.

MacLure, M., & French, P. (1981). A comparison of talk at home and at school. In C.G. Wells (Ed.), *Learning through interaction: The study of language development* (pp. 205–239). Cambridge, UK: Cambridge University Press.

MacWhinney, B. (1995). *The CHILDES Project: Tools for analyzing talk.* Hillsdale, NJ: Erlbaum.

MacWhinney, B., & Snow, C. (1990). The Child Language Data Exchange System: An update. *Journal of Child Language, 12,* 457–472.

Mannle, S., & Tomasello, M. (1987). Fathers, siblings, and the bridge hypothesis. In K.E. Nelson & A. van Kleeck (Eds.), *Children's Language* (Vol. VI). Hillsdale, NJ: Erlbaum.

Newport, E.L. (1977). Motherese: The speech of mothers to young children. In N.J. Castellan, D.B. Pisoni, & G.R. Potts (Eds.), *Cognitive theory* (Vol. II). Hillsdale, NJ: Erlbaum.

Ninio, A., & Bruner, J. (1978). The achievement and antecedents of labelling. *Journal of Child Language, 5,* 1–15.

Richards, B.J. (1990). Access to the agenda: Some observations on language development research and its relevance for the practitioner. *Australian Journal of Remedial Education, 22,* 16–20.

Richards, B.J., & Gallaway, C. (1999). Language acquisition in children: Input and interaction. In B. Spolsky (Ed.), *Concise encyclopedia of educational linguistics.* Oxford, UK: Pergamon.

Sinclair, J., & Coulthard, M. (1975). *Towards an analysis of discourse.* Oxford, UK: Oxford University Press.

Snow, B., & Goldfield, B. (1983). Turn the page please: Situation-specific language acquisition. *Journal of Child Language, 10,* 551–569.

Speidel, G., & Nelson, K.E. (Eds.). (1989). *The many faces of imitation in language learning.* New York: Springer-Verlag.

Stubbs, M. (1975). Teaching and talking: A sociolinguistic approach to classroom interaction. In G. Chanon & S. Delamont (Eds.), *Frontiers of classroom research.* Slough, UK: National Foundation for Educational Research.

Tizard, B., & Hughes, M. (1984). *Young children learning: Talking and thinking at home and at school.* London: Fontana.

Waterland, L. (1985). *Read with me: An apprenticeship approach to reading.* Stroud, UK: Thimble Press.

Wells, C.G. (Ed.). (1981). *Learning through interaction: The study of language development.* Cambridge, UK: Cambridge University Press.

Wells, C.G. (1986). *The meaning makers: Children learning language and using language to learn.* Portsmouth, NH: Heinemann.

Westgate, D., & Hughes, M. (1997). Identifying "quality" in classroom talk. *Language and Education, 11,* 125–130.

## For Further Reading

Gallaway, C., & Richards, B.J. (Eds.). (1994). *Input and interaction in language acquisition.* Cambridge, UK: Cambridge University Press.

Geekie, P., & Raban, B. (1994). Language learning at home and at school. In C. Gallaway & B.J. Richards (Eds.), *Input and interaction in language acquisition.* Cambridge, UK: Cambridge University Press.

Greenhough, P., & Hughes, M. (1998). Parents' and teachers' interventions in children's reading. *British Educational Research Journal, 24,* 383–398.

Grugeon, E., Hubbard, L., Smith, C., & Dawes, L. (1998). *Teaching speaking and listening in the primary school.* London: David Fulton.

Hughes, M., & Greenough, P. (1999). Encouraging conversing: Trying to change what parents do when their children read with them. *Reading, 33,* 98–105.

Reynolds, B. (1997). *Literacy in the pre-school: The roles of teachers and parents.* Stoke on Trent, UK: Trentham.

Whitehead, M. (1999). *Supporting language and literacy development.* Buckingham, UK: Open University Press.

Williams, A., & Gregory, E. (1999). Home and school reading practices in two East End communities. In A. Tosi & C. Leung (Eds.), *Rethinking language education.* London: Centre for Information on Language Teaching and Research.

# Assessing Student Language Growth: Kirsten's Profile

*Patrick Griffin and Patricia G. Smith*

It is near the end of the school year for Kirsten and the others in her Grade 5/6 classroom. These 11- and 12-year-olds and their teacher, Anne, have been together for 2 years learning in a classroom awash with purposeful talk—a classroom where all have been constructing themselves as learners who take charge of their lives. Kirsten is holding the attention of the large group as she finishes reading a book report on Gary Crew's (1992) novel *Lucy's Bay*:

> You can understand why Sam doesn't want to go back to the red rocks. If I had been looking after my sister and had gone away for a minute and when I got back and she was gone, I wouldn't want to go back there. Life goes on even if your loved ones leave. Sometimes you have to just forget about the past and concentrate on the future. Just because you may have killed someone (well you think so) it really isn't your fault. I can relate to it because my grandpa died and I try not to think about it, but I do. The seeds where the wind blows them away is a sort of sign that life goes on and new life starts. The only reason why Mum, Dad and Grandpa could go and see the marble carving by the rocks is that Sam really thinks that it was his fault, and they want to help him deal with the experience.

Then Kirsten speaks about her learning:

> I chose this book report from my Journal to read to you today. I hadn't realized how I was using extra information from the pictures and watching for the patterns and that I had gone on thinking after the talking. When I wrote about the seeds being a symbol of new life I thought that was important and yet I hadn't talked about that in our group discussion after the book reading. It also shows that there is more than one main idea in this book but they are all intertwined. There is the one about life going on and one about expecting too much of little kids and about making fresh starts and not being cast down by the past. Gary Crew wasn't straight out about what had happened so we had a few puzzles to sort out.
>
> This is why I think the best part of the reading is when we talk and argue about it all. Gary Crew is one of my favorite authors because there is so much to think about when you read him. Also Greg Rogers is an absolutely brilliant artist who makes his painting give you a real feeling about the beach and what it was like. I plan to do an author and an illustrator study about them next term because there is still more to investigate.

A s observers we can make judgments about learning. We can infer that Kirsten and her classmates have learned that meaning does not reside exclusively in a text. They have learned how to transact with texts and make meaning out of the web of meaning in themselves and in the text; that meaning is not fixed but is open and dependent on a number of elements, including context and culture. Kirsten, making inferences from what has been accepted as learning, shows us that she is able to assess her own growth and to make her own judgments.

## A New Assessment Framework

A fundamental purpose of assessment is to predict or infer progress in learning from a basis of bounded and contextualized evidence to an unbounded and generalized set of circumstances. In doing this, Kirsten's teacher, like all teachers, often has to put her professional judgment on the line publicly. In making an explicit judgment and declaring the criteria, the teacher exposes the basis of decisions to public scrutiny. There is nothing wrong with this—it is common to make judgments and state them publicly, but in these circumstances the basis of the decision is also open to scrutiny.

This judgment cannot be transferred to an instrument, because no instrument, task, or assessment process can ever predict from the specific to the general. This is the role of the teacher—the person who manages the learning process, conducts the assessment, and interprets the observations of students' performances and gives them meaning in a learning context. Without this attribution of meaning, an assessment is a meaningless process.

There have been many attempts to use teacher judgment in assessment in a way that gives credibility to the teacher and provides useable information to parents, to other teachers, and to students. We have seen checklists, tests, projects, and portfolios among many other approaches. Each assessment approach provides its own data and approach to interpreting specific observations of student language, and most teachers use a combination of these approaches. What has been needed is a framework that helps to bring them all together.

Griffin, Smith, and Burrill (1995) created Literacy Profiles as a framework for teachers to use to interpret systematic observations of student language. In simple terms, a profile is a scale consisting of descriptions that taken together depict progress in learning. Griffin et al. present what is essentially a criterion-referenced framework for interpreting observations of students' classroom language behavior. Monitoring language over increasing levels of growth is consistent with the definition of criterion referencing offered by Glaser (1981), which "involves the development of procedures whereby assessments of proficiency could be referred to stages along progressions of increasing competence" (p. 935). The combination of criterion referencing and Rasch (1960) approaches used in the development of profiles (based on the work of Griffin, 1989) allows for a more objective interpretation of growth. An essential feature of a student's profile is that it provides the evidence that a teacher needs to defend judgments of student growth in learning. The illustrations presented in this study show how important this task is, how the observer interacts with the evidence of growth, and how important it is to have a framework in which to interpret the evidence.

Griffin and Nix (1991) defined assessment and reporting in much the same way—observing, recording, interpreting, and communicating. In this discussion we present examples of both observation and inference. Profiles provided the interpretive framework that enabled us to put our, and the teacher's, observations into perspective and to generalize about the language growth exhibited by the children.

The idea of inferring language growth is important. We cannot directly observe growth in language. We infer it from our observations of student language behavior and make inferences about growth. Messick (1984) argued that validity of assessment was inextricably linked to the inference, not the process. According to Griffin and Nix (1991) inference is assisted by interpretive frameworks. They argued that profiles help teachers in making inferences and hence in improving the validity of assessment. What follows is an example of the process of recording observations, referring them to a framework of increasing development, and inferring language growth.

## Methods of Observation and Inference

Observing children interacting with each other and with a teacher is a rich source of evidence for language assessment opportunity without a need for structured instruments or intrusive procedures. Observing in a naturalistic setting provides an ideal opportunity for monitoring and assessing language growth. Profiles of language growth helped Kirsten's teacher to guide her observations and placed her in a good position from which inferences of language development and use could be made.

The Literacy Profiles have been used in many different countries including the United States, Canada, Australia, New Zealand, and Ireland. Translations of the profiles have been used in Cambodia and in Egypt. They are published by Heinemann as *The American Literacy Profiles*. The new edition due to be published in 2001 will have a more generic title. Anne, an Australian teacher, chose to use them because they offer so much of a rich framework within which to interpret observations of student work.

Literature groups were constructed at the beginning of the school year by the teacher, Anne, in accordance with the belief that as part of a reading community students develop and refine responses as they share the interpretation of text with one another and make regular acquaintance with authors and illustrators (Langer, 1990). We surmised that these groups would be a rich source of data for an investigation of the nature of talk in the classroom. There has been widespread interest in the way that conversations between adults and young children, and among the children themselves, contribute to spoken-language development (see Barnes, Britton, & Torbe, 1986; Dickinson, 1993; Peterson, 1992); but very little interest has been shown in what would seem to be a similar relationship, the influence of this talk on reading development.

We describe various observations of Kirsten and the other students engaged in purposeful talk over the Grade 5/6 years and link inferences about Kirsten's language development to the profiles. In the same way that all teachers intuitively make inferences, Kirsten's teacher links inferences to the profiles as an example of the application of an interpretive framework. They are used to place Kirsten on a profile scale so the growth that has taken place is made explicit. In the profile scales shown in Figure 1, the statements presented in bold indicate the behaviors that the teacher could observe in the large- and small-group talk about texts. Of course, it is difficult to separate these speaking and listening indicators from reading indicators, so some of the reading indicators were italicized and included in the Speaking and Listening bands of the profiles. How the teacher was able to translate the observed speech to the indicators will be shown in the following discussion.

## Beginning the Dialogue

The dialogue in this section shows Kirsten as she progresses through Grade 5 and Grade 6 in a multiage classroom. The speech acts in book discussions are the particular focus. To begin, it is important to take time to review what talk was like early on in Grade 5. The following text is an excerpt from a literature-group session using self-chosen books in small groups. Anne had allocated turns for Matthew, Max, Stacey, Kirsten, Stephanie, and Angus. It is here that Kirsten is heard, though barely, taking her turn at being a good student.

| | |
|---|---|
| Max: | I read John Marsden, *Out of Time*, and it's about this boy called James who finds this crooked time machine that (indistinct) was creating in the lab and at the moment he's just found out how to use it and he went all dizzy at one point because there's a magnetic force field being used. |
| Kirsten: | Why did he make a magnetic force field? |
| Max: | Because he wanted a pocket time machine. |

---

## FIGURE 1
## Band speaking and listening

**D USES OF LANGUAGE**
**Tells personal anecdotes, illustrating in a relevant way the issue being discussed. Recounts a story** or repeats a song spontaneously. Retells scenes from a film or drama. **Offers predictions about what will come next.** Recites poems. **Asks questions in conversation. Has a second try at something to make it more precise. Arouses and maintains an audience's interest during formal presentations. Asks for explanation or repetition if meaning is unclear.**

Features of language
**Uses a range of vocabulary related to a particular topic. Maintains receptive body stance in conversation. Speaks in a way that conveys feelings (while keeping emotions under control).**

**E USES OF LANGUAGE**
**Presents a point of view to an audience. Is interested in another's point of view.** Presents materials with consideration for audience needs. **Speculates and puts forward a tentative proposition. Uses logic, arguments, or appeals to feelings to persuade others.** Explores concepts related to concrete materials by describing, narrating, or explaining how things work and why things happen. Dramatizes familiar stories, showing understanding. Uses convincing dialogue to role play short scenes involving familiar situations or emotions. **Invites others to participate. Takes initiative in raising new aspects of an issue. Asks questions to elicit more from an individual.** Answers questions confidently and clearly in interviews. Asks for the meaning of familiar words used in unfamiliar ways.

Features of language
**Makes links between ideas in discussions.** Uses complex connectives in speech, such as "although," "in spite of," "so that." **Uses syntactical structures—principal and subordinate clauses. Uses vocabulary appropriate to audience and purpose.** Distinguishes among words of similar meanings.

Interest and attitudes (Reading profile)
*Recommends books to others.*

**F USES OF LANGUAGE**
Asks speaker to clarify ambiguities. Asks questions about words of similar meanings. **Elicits information or reaction or opinions of others in conversation. Asks questions to draw information from the group. Indicates disagreement in a constructive manner.** Attempts to resolve disagreement or misunderstanding. **Supports constructively the statements of others. Attempts to keep discussion on the topic.** Makes formal introductions with courtesy and clarity. Tells a story with expression and emphasis, showing confidence, highlighting key points, and demonstrating the storyteller's art. **Explores abstract ideas (justice, good, and evil) by generalizing, hypothesizing, or inferring.** Improvises in role play, drawing on a range of texts.

Features of language
Uses a range of idiomatic expressions with confidence. Reacts to an inappropriate choice of words. **Makes positive interjections.**

**G USES OF LANGUAGE**
Asks interview questions that are relevant. Extends another group member's contribution by elaboration or illustration. **Helps others to put forward ideas.** Summarizes the conclusions reached in a group

*(continued)*

---

**FIGURE 1**
**Band speaking and listening (continued)**

---

**G USES OF LANGUAGE** (continued)
discussion. Asks speakers for background information. Dramatizes scenes from complex stories, showing understanding of dramatic structure. Role plays/improvises shaped scenes, showing understanding of dramatic structure. **Talks about response/meaning of text.**

Features of language
Uses new words spontaneously. Varies tone, pitch, and pace of speech to create effect and aid communication. Self-corrects to remove the effects on audience of a poor choice of words. Comments on some ways in which spoken language differs from written language (e.g., repetitions, colloquialisms, slang, emphasis, incomplete utterances). Talks about special forms of language such as accents or dialects in a positive way.

Responses (from Reading profile)
**Describes links between personal experience and arguments and ideas about text. Makes connections among texts, recognizing similarities of themes and values. Discusses author's intent for the reader.** *Discusses styles used by different authors.* **Offers reasons for the feelings provoked by a text.** *Discusses a range of interpretations of text. Offers critical opinion or analysis of reading passages in discussion. Justifies own appraisal of a text.*

---

Reading bands D, E, F, and G. *The American literacy profile scales.*

---

| | |
|---|---|
| Kirsten: | How does the pocket time machine work? |
| Max: | I don't know how to explain. The pocket time machine was as big as a calculator. |
| Stacey: | Who's the main character? |
| Max: | James. |
| Matthew: | How old is he? |
| Max: | About my age. |
| Angus: | Who's the author? |
| Max: | John Marsden. |

The students had developed a formula for book-sharing sessions: They asked ritualistic questions that were repeated occasionally. Max gave the name of the author and then Angus again asked the formulaic question, "Who's the author?" Kirsten asked a more in-depth question but Max answered cursorily. All the speaking turns could be described as monologic. There were no real conversations. These exchanges reflected the initiate-response-feedback patterns often apparent in classroom talk. The students had established a framework for book discussion: Somebody described the plot, sometimes there was a minor clarification question, somebody asked about the author, and somebody asked about the main character. We learned nothing about their meaning-making in reading, but the conversation showed that they had begun to form a procedure for examining texts without developing their response to the text.

What assessment can be made? Anne can highlight a Band D indicator and start to build a description of Kirsten's growth using examples of her work on the book discussions. Indicators in earlier bands will already have been highlighted in previous years. Bands A, B, and C formed a general description of Kirsten as she entered Grade 5. These statements of growth are summarized in nutshell statements that accompany each band (see Figure 2). The nutshells are short descriptions of the behaviors in each Band. They help teachers decide the bands on which to focus their observations. Her question "Why did he make a magnetic force field?" in the previous discussion clearly falls within the

---

**FIGURE 2**
**Nutshell statements**

---

**G**
Uses language increasingly to explore ideas, question, and summarize discussions. Uses new words spontaneously. Varies tone, pitch, pace of speech to create effect and aid communication. Explores and reflects on ideas while listening; is becoming familiar with a range of spoken forms of language and is able to distinguish between them for purpose, meaning, and appropriate audience.

**F**
Can persuade and influence peers, using language. Clarifies and orders thoughts in conversation. Shows expression of ideas, feelings, opinions, and ability to generalize or hypothesize. Speech contains inferences drawn from varied situations. Links stories and spoken forms of language to values. Is aware of relevance and irrelevance, pitch intensity, and intonation.

**E**
Uses logic, argument, and questioning to clarify ideas and understanding appropriate to audience and purpose. Accepts others' opinions and is developing listening strategies listening for relationships in stories.

**D**
Can recount and retell, recite with felling, and use a range of vocabulary to arouse and maintain audience interest. Distinguishes between social and informational listening and will seek clarification.

**C**
Is developing confidence with spoken language. Is sensitive to voice control in specific situations. Is developing confidence through active listening, responding, and clarifying when meaning is not clear.

**B**
Experiments and uses language in a variety of ways, including clarifying ideas and experiences. Body language assists in conveying understanding. Listens for a range of purposes, discriminates sounds in words, and can recall stories told.

**A**
Understands social conventions of spoken language and responds appropriately. Listens attentively, interacts with the speaker, and responds with interest.

range of Band D's Features of Language, specifically "Uses a range of vocabulary suitable to a topic."

## Limiting Teacher Talk

Teacher dominance of talk is a well-known and powerful phenomenon. In the previous discussion the students had developed a format using formulaic questions as an appropriate way to organize discussion. How did they learn to do this? A number of studies have identified a characteristic initiate-respond-feedback-exchange structure as the basic unit of discourse in most lessons, especially those involving large groups of students (Mehan, 1979a, 1979b; O'Flahavan, Hartman, & Pearson, 1988). In such exchanges the teacher initiates the interaction and provides the feedback. The student, for the most part, plays the role of respondent. Most teachers, however, are not aware that they dominate discussions and that their students follow this pattern in their talk.

The following example is taken from a discussion session early in Grade 5.

| Teacher: | But what sort of character is he? |
|---|---|
| Angus: | Mean and old. |
| Amber: | He wants you to make all these deals like that if he's.... |
| Teacher: | Why is he interested in making the deals though? |
| Kirsten: | Because all he probably cares about is the underground. |
| Daniel: | It's his, he wants this and he wants that. |
| Luke: | He's sort of a mean and old person because some old people are… |
| Teacher: | Why is he so involved with the underground? |
| Luke: | Because he thinks that that's the only good place, he doesn't think that… |
| Teacher: | Why is it so important to him? |

In this exchange, the teacher asked the questions and so led the discussion. This discourse implies that Anne knew what the "correct" responses would be and her questions often required the students to display knowledge that she already possessed. They were not "need-to-know" questions. The knowledge expected of the readers was text-based and the students were not heard to be engaged in making new meanings. They demonstrated a process and a fixed pattern of analysis of the text without a discernible response. The only indicator Anne was able to highlight for Kirsten from the exchange was the Band D indicator "Maintains receptive body stance in conversation."

When Anne listened to the audiotape she was horrified to hear how much she was controlling the talk. She heard herself organizing discussions by giving turns and monitoring behavior. This typical classroom behavior needed to be changed if the students were to have the real conversations that would develop their speaking and listening growth further. Anne decided she would step back and allow the students to take responsibility for their own behavior.

### New Learning Strategies

Anne made use of several strategies to encourage students to reconstruct and interpret literary texts for themselves without her leading the discussion. Wertsch's (1991) claim, following Vygotsky (1987), that dialogic interaction is critical to internalizing social languages was the underlying theory for the emphasis on student discussion, but a pattern of discourse needed to be established that supported this dialogic interaction. Aidan Chambers (1993) designed the Tell Me strategy to scaffold learners so that they could take on learning by themselves, and this strategy became a useful way of mediating learning during the year. (See Chapter 2, page 18 for a further explanation of *scaffolding*.) Chambers' strategy of using patterns, and thus symbols, gave the students a way into meaningful talk about text which was not able to emerge until the classroom procedures were changed to allow for student response.

Anne read the picture book *John Brown, Rose and the Midnight Cat* (Wagner & Brooks, 1977) to the students and had them brainstorm their responses under the headings "I like," "I dislike," "Patterns," and "Puzzles" and connect their responses across the columns. These connections were discussed briefly in a large group before the students chose the connection they wished to discuss in small groups. The students' discussion would then be driven by the need to report back to the large group, including the teacher, when their ideas would be used for further exploration.

Using the profiles as a guide, Anne had a genuine opportunity to observe language behavior and make inferences about the children's language development. Interactions provided the raw data for making those inferences. Together with Anne, we hypothesized that work in small groups without the teacher would allow the students to test their initial responses within these secure confines. They would be able to clarify and refine their responses and obtain the confirmations they needed to develop trust in their intuitions and the relevance of their experience. Students were expected to carry on the usual practices of a conversation including taking part without putting up their hands for a turn. It was hoped that evidence would appear of the students deliberately using the ways to talk about literature to which they been introduced.

## Kirsten's Profile Expands

In the following discussion about *John Brown, Rose and The Midnight Cat*, the students picked up on someone's puzzle about whether the dog was in the dead husband's place and was acting like a husband. From the language used it can be inferred that the children were using patterns and symbols to express meaning.

Kirsten:     I think that John Brown was jealous of the Midnight Cat because Rose liked the cat and she liked the dog and she wanted both and he thought no one could know Rose better than he could.

Amber:     I reckon she was tricking him.

Matthew:     I agree with Amber. At the start when John Brown said "no," in the picture she sort of went like that. She could have been tricking so the dog knows that she loves them both as much.

Elizabeth:     But I think the pictures with the dog were sort of to make him sit on the seat 'cause it really did look like her husband.

Hayley:     I couldn't imagine him in clothes.

Amber:     I could.

In the next excerpt, the students started to develop the idea that the midnight cat was a symbol of death, independent from the teacher or any teacher suggestions. Kirsten made a connection that has been made by some literary critics.

Elizabeth:     So he's protecting her. He doesn't want her to die.

Kirsten:     And the cat was a symbol of death or whatever, like when he tipped the milk over you could see only a shadow.

Elizabeth:     It never showed its face.

The possibility of the cat symbolizing death involved analysis of the story line, but in doing that analysis the students were led to make explicit the clues they found to tell if something was used as a sign. Kirsten's responses were no longer formulaic, but began to represent her point of view rather than a set and established process. Her response to the text was emerging, and the teacher added new indicators from Bands E and F.

**Band E.**
Presents a point of view to an audience.

I think that John Brown was jealous of the Midnight Cat because Rose liked the cat and she liked the dog and she wanted both and he thought no one could know Rose better than he could.

**Band F.**
Explores abstract ideas.

And the cat was a symbol of death or whatever, like when he tipped the milk over you could see only a shadow.

There were often examples of students expressing dislike for elements of the story that they found difficult to understand. Here is a discussion about *The Lake at the End of the World* (Macdonald, 1993):

| Max: | Well when they closed the entrance, then…How would Hector get out? They must have had another entrance. They must have made another one to get supplies. |
| Amber: | But didn't Diana pick him up with the dog? |
| Max: | Yes, but that was after they found he was going outside. |
| Kirsten: | What I want to know is, if they don't want the people who live underground to go out, why did they have the maze in the first place? |
| Amber: | Yes, it is silly, isn't it? |
| Max: | Maybe they need to get supplies. |
| Kirsten: | Yes. It's silly 'cause no one's allowed out. Hector wouldn't have been able to go out if he didn't have Stuart, so I don't know. |

The students expressed their puzzlement in such comments as "It's silly" or "I can't understand why she did that." If the comment was taken up and discussed and an explanation was suggested, an agreement or "agreement to disagree" was reached of what the text meant to that group of readers at that particular time. One-dimensional responses were left behind and a more elaborate reaction to the text emerged far beyond the formulaic responses described earlier. Responses now incorporated others' points of view and the teacher was able to add some more Band F indicators to Kirsten's profile.

**Band F.**
Elicits information or reaction or opinions of others' conversation.

Asks questions to draw information from the group.

Indicates disagreement in a constructive manner.

What I want to know is, if they don't want the people who live underground to go out, why did they have the maze in the first place?

Yes. It's silly 'cause no one's allowed out. Hector wouldn't have been able to go out if he didn't have Stuart, so I don't know.

In these early stages not all students were good at taking up others' puzzles for discussion. Kirsten was one of the first to persist in trying to have her puzzles discussed. However, they were all becoming confident about expressing their puzzles to others. They had become risk-takers in a safe situation. In these first sessions some of the students were already becoming part of a student-to-student dialogue by actively attending to the responses of others.

# Readers and Thinkers

The following is an excerpt from a discussion by the group that shows how they began to conduct natural conversations as they built on each other's responses. They treated each other as thinkers, following the patterns of thought and action that had been encouraged previously when the teacher used the Tell Me strategy. The students accepted that they were to work through their own understandings when the teacher showed by keeping out of the discussion that she was interested in the students' responses rather than in predetermined interpretations.

Amber:    How did she know what happened to the guy inside the water?

Stephanie:    Probably just another myth.

Kirsten:    It was about the man who couldn't get any sun and he went to drown himself and he saw all the blood and when he came out he was dead and he couldn't do anything.

Max:    So that was the first myth and this one.... What about the monster?

Angus:    I thought it was a fish in waders that was catching him instead of him catching it.

It became evident that extended discourse in social interactions allowed the students to acquire the cognitive and linguistic operations used in the construction of new texts. Students were supported to engage in the process of literary understanding, exploring, rethinking, explaining, and defending their own understandings. They thought about their thinking in different ways and became responsible for how they would transact with text, as the following dialogue shows.

Stephanie:    And you're talking about it in groups so it makes you understand it more.

Kirsten:    The talk helps you think.

Stephanie:    Because you talk it over with your group and you're just telling them questions and they answer and then you just talk. Answers instead of questions. Some days I talk a lot and other times I don't.

Kirsten:    Because sometimes you just sit there and you think, "I want to know if someone's going to ask that question," and then you sort of say...you think, "That's a silly question for me to ask. I know the answer now."

There were two clear patterns that emerged in Kirsten's responses that were characteristic of this particular group. All the students were adamant that they had learned that talking was part of reading. They contrasted their new confidence in discussion, and their increasing ability to live in text worlds that changed as they read and talked, with their previous lessons when they answered questions about main characters and the theme of the narrative at the conclusion of a text reading. There are indicators in Band E that reflect this kind of talk and the teacher was able to highlight two of them.

> The talk helps you think.
>
> Because sometimes you just sit there and you think, "I want to know if someone's going to ask that question," and then you sort of say…you think, "That's a silly question for me to ask. I know the answer now.

**Band E.**
Takes initiative in raising new aspects of an issue.

Makes links between ideas in discussion.

In an attempt to reflect on their thinking processes the students used a metaphor of "pictures in the mind." They appeared to have adapted this concept to settings where they were asked to function individually. Kirsten described her thinking by saying, "I don't really get just pictures in my head. It's like a proper movie. You've got this screen and you get it all. It's all your thoughts." The students' descriptions often matched Vygotskian views about inner speech as the intermediate or transactional form of thinking—speaking that has its own speeded up movement, its own peculiar syntax, semantics, and pragmatics. It is like speech without words and is almost beyond consciousness, but it plays an important role in helping students to prepare for specific kinds of utterances. Vygotsky (1971) referred to this development of speech as "imaging" because the reader/thinker uses images on which to temporarily project thoughts, words, even entire texts in a very fast time. Later on in Grade 6, Kirsten and Stephanie reflected this imaging as they talked about their reading and what they had learned.

| Kirsten: | I sort of know I've improved because I sort of understand books more than I used to because when you read before in Grade 4 you thought reading a book was reading a book and finding out what happens but now I sort of understand that you get pictures in your mind. You talk to yourself while you are reading and you talk to other people. |
|---|---|
| Stephanie: | Because sometimes the author's making puzzles for you to answer, and we keep finding different answers. |
| Kirsten: | Once I would start to read a lot of boring books. Now I know not many books are boring because you've got to get into them to actually like them, because some books might have a boring first chapter and then maybe the second and… |
| Stephanie: | The rest is real good. |
| Kirsten: | It stops being boring because you're into it and if you start the first few pages that are really hard to understand, well you don't understand that and then when you get into the book, like say two more chapters after that, it's really coming to you and your mind is busy. |

Stephanie:     It's like *The Lake at the End of the World*, when we started that I thought, "This is a boring book. We're not going to enjoy this," and then we started to have puzzles and notice the patterns and we sort of understood it a bit more after we talked all that out. I started to think about these while I was listening and after that it sort of got really good and you wanted to keep reading.

The students in this group could be observed using reading as inner speech. As they read and talked they were controlling and regulating meaning, and thus in the transaction were creating new meaning. The three separate utterances by Kirsten in this conversation allowed for the highlighting of new indicators showing Kirsten consolidating Band E and also moving further into Band F.

**Band F.**
Explores abstract ideas.

**Band E.**
Presents a point of view to an audience.

Speculates and puts forward a tentative proposition.

**Band E.**
Makes links between ideas in discussion.

Uses syntactical structures-principal and subordinate clauses.

Speculates and puts forward a tentative proposition.

I sort of know I've improved because I sort of understand books more than I used to because when you read before in Grade 4 you thought reading a book was reading a book and finding out what happens. But now I sort of understand that you get pictures in your mind.

You talk to yourself while you are reading and you talk to other people.

Kirsten has learned to take her part in conversation and now there are many opportunities for the teacher to highlight her growth as a learner.

Once I would start to read a lot of boring books.

Now I know not many books are boring because you've got to get into them to actually like them,

because some books might have a boring first chapter and then maybe the second and…Then it stops being boring because you're into it.

Several indicators could be applied to these utterances. This reinforces for the teacher that Kirsten is able to be described by the Band E nutshell statement (see Figure 2). We know that learning does not take place step by step along a set continuum. Kirsten demonstrates that she can generally be described as consolidating one set of behaviors while showing some in the next set and maybe finishing one or two in a previous set.

As reading became internalized, it acted as a kind of inner speech that was a draft for further meaning-making, or transactions, with the text. Following Bakhtin (1981), students talked of the noise and the voices in their heads. This notion of inner speaking and the students' regulation of it is very exciting. These students did speak in their minds, were aware they did, and used this knowledge to regulate their thinking.

| Stephanie: | It's interesting that people think different things. Sometimes you think that a pattern is going to be for this and other people think it's going to be for that and it's interesting to find out what other people are thinking because you've got different things and pictures—what the characters look like and why they do it and all that. |
|---|---|
| Kirsten: | Yes, and after you've heard people, you think this and they think that and you think some things they thought and you sort of join up all what's going on in your head. |

On the surface this speech is not so sophisticated but Kirsten is showing some consolidation of Band F outcomes.

> Yes, and after you've heard people, you think this and they think that and you think some things they thought and you sort of join up all what's going on in your head.

**Band F.**
Supports
constructively the
statements of others.

Makes positive
interjections.

## Considering Growth

Growth is evident over the period of time that these observations occurred, as Anne allowed the students to explore, conjecture, and draw out inferences from their own and their classmates' views. The small-group discussions had allowed the students to take control and regulate their own behavior. The students were learning how to be participants in discussion about books in this classroom as they developed their knowledge of literature and control of their mental processes, and this showed in the profiles. This awareness and understanding of their own cognitive processes was highlighted when the students put them into action when transacting with texts. These students realized that they were not passive receptacles of information, but that their minds were active construction agents of meaning. When the students insisted that reading was also talk, they demonstrated understanding that meaning was constructed socially. They were all following their own paths to learning within the social and cultural context of this classroom.

In their talk the students grappled with the idea that thoughts are not just words but something deep from the imagination. Discussion in a literature circle of Chris Van Allsburg's *Polar Express* (1985) demonstrated these struggles.

| Kirsten: | *The Polar Express* is like the ocean liner in *The Mysteries of Harris Burdick*. There it appears, smack in the middle of town. I kept thinking, "What does this mean? Why the train?" |
|---|---|
| Max: | It's to shock you. A train seems so ordinary but next thing, there we are, off to the North Pole. And who to see? Santa Claus. |

Elizabeth: But it's a kind of scary Santa. The colors are so dark and that picture where he was giving his speech to the elves. He seemed to be threatening them. It's like what you said about *Jumanji*, Max.

Max: Gruesome.

Kirsten: You know how we think about Santa as a jolly fellow with all his elves happily making presents? Well this slavery probably is what it would be like in his workshop if they did really make all the things. They would have to be flat out like a sweatshop. I kept getting pictures of them miserably working in the toy factory.

Max: I kept thinking all through the book about the speech scene where Santa gets them going. It's like old pictures of Hitler giving a speech. We think we are seeing news but Van Allsburg is making us realize they we aren't seeing properly. On the other hand look at the thick white borders..

Daniel: (interrupting) You always look for borders ever since we had [a discussion] about Max in *Where the Wild Things Are* starting with borders and then the pictures filling up the page when we were inside his head for the rumpus.

Max: Well it's my book [Because his name is Max, too]. But Sendak started a good idea. It works so many times.

Kirsten: Do you think he meant us to worry about the point of the Santa Claus story. He isn't true. Be careful!

Amber: Yeah. He wants to make us think about it. I kept trying things in my mind. Trying to sort out what he was trying to make me think it is all about us wanting things at someone else's expense. Write that down, Max. (Max was scribe for the small-group report to the whole class that session.)

In this dialogue about the illustrated books, Kirsten gives information, seeks information through a question, and offers advice ("Be careful!"). The grammar is the tool Kirsten uses to think and feel. She uses grammar to make meaning and not just to act as a conduit for her ideas. She sets the tenor of the speech (see Halliday, Chapter 1, p. 6) when she asks a rhetorical question, "Do you think he meant us to worry about the point of the Santa Claus story?" She answers it herself: "He isn't true." Then she warns her listeners, "Be careful!" It is when students learn this grammar of speech, which is different from that of writing, that through debate, conversation, and argument they will become critical learners, having mastered the speech genres of their culture. Because these students have been given ample opportunity for purposeful talk, they have grown as users of language. Kirsten's teacher is now able to highlight more indicators to show that she is moving very quickly into more sophisticated talk as shown by Band G indicators and the consolidation of Band F.

*The Polar Express* is like the ocean liner in *The Mysteries of Harris Burdick*. There it appears, smack in the middle of town I kept thinking, "What does this mean? Why the train?"

Do you think he meant us to worry about the point of the Santa Claus story?

Well this slavery probably is what it would be in his workshop if they did really make all the things. They would have to be flat out like a sweatshop.

**Band G.**
Makes connections betweeen texts, recognizing similarities of themes and values.

Talks about response/ meaning of text.

Discusses author's intent for the reader.

**Band F.**
Explores abstract ideas like justice, good and evil by generalizing, hypothesizing or inferring.

## How The Profiles Help to Monitor This Growth

The profiles shown here have helped the teacher to interpret evidence of Kirsten's increasing competence. Anne does not have to rely on any course content or any instruments of measurement. What is achieved is described explicitly, making it a simple task for her to interpret the learning, to synthesize her judgment, and to make inferences about language development. It can be as simple for her as using a highlighter on the appropriate indicators. These indicators do not define any exhaustive or compulsory set of behaviors but rather typify an indicative set of behaviors that are demonstrated at each Band level. They highlight positive achievements.

As we saw in Figure 2, the nutshell statements attached to each band help the teacher express an overall impression as a basis for inferring language growth. The profiles provide a way of interpreting change and making generalizations or inferences about a construct called "language development" rather than measuring it. Profiles have put the teacher in the position of the assessment instrument using the actual student performance as the assessment task. The process of compiling profile data can be of formative use in that it may help the teaching and learning process if the teacher notes that certain indicators have not been considered in her curriculum.

# Talking of Change: A Cautionary Conclusion

The profiles were used because it was important to find a way of interpreting the observations of change in such a way that the pertinent outcomes of the curriculum in use in Kirsten's classroom were reflected. In order to make inferences and then defensible statements about growth, it was also necessary to show how this led to changes in students. But there are a lot of givens in such an approach. Kirsten and her classmates definitely changed. There were no doubts in the teacher's or our minds about that. There was no doubt in Kirsten's mind either.

Often however, the intuition of feeling that change has occurred is not enough. If we are to examine change, growth, learning, effectiveness, or differences, then we must also have an idea of the construct we are observing. That is, if Kirsten has changed, exactly *what* has changed and *how* would we communicate this change to others? More importantly, if we are monitoring change, how do we know where to intervene to promote further growth? Once we determine what has changed, how can we determine in what direction and by how much has she changed? Has she changed more than we might have expected? Has she changed in relative terms more or less than her classmates? It is impossible to even talk about change if there is no meaningful direction to the change. We could talk about a broad spectrum of learning and count the outcomes before and after, but that completely surrenders the issue of comparability of outcomes over time or among individuals. This is the role we chose for the profiles. They provide the framework for interpreting the size and direction of change in students' achievement, and for inferring change in terms of a language construct, but they do not give a precise estimate of the amount of change.

As we learned at the beginning of this chapter, teachers understand change and direction in students' learning. They use this intuitive understanding of change to plan curricula and to develop materials that suit contiguous age groups. As Kirsten and other students illustrate new insights into change and growth, we need to have an adaptable system that can accommodate the changes and incorporate them into such systems as profiles. The thing that must remain constant is the opportunity to observe and infer learning. Profiles are a framework that helps teachers do this. Kirsten and her classmates provided the evidence, we observed their performances, and then referred the observations to the profiles to help us understand the nature of their change. That is assessment. Whether is it authentic, standardized, dimensional, or any other form of assessment does not really matter.

We accept that our standards referencing system (profiles) is not perfect. We can usually reference to a norm (defined by our knowledge in terms of our expectations of the class or social group) or to a criterion scale (defined by our knowledge of a discipline such as literacy), but these can change over time. Criterion interpretation scales such as the profiles will change as we improve our understanding of learning and knowledge of reading and spoken language.

Controlling the influence of an observer of the evidence is still problematic. At best we can control it by applying principles of task design or by providing structured ways of interpreting observations. At worst we ignore it and allow the observations to dominate and become reified through numbers, classifications, and categories with labels that take on a social, educational, and economic significance far beyond their worth. However, as we have seen, criterion-referenced interpretation frameworks hold great promise in allowing for more objective interpretations of growth.

# Conclusion

Using Kirsten as our exemplar, this study has been an examination of the change in and growth of students' speaking and listening skills in the context of a reading program. Our focus has been on Kirsten as she responded to literature, and how all the readers used talk to develop sophistication in their dialogue and their thinking. Part of this focus has been on the teacher, who valued her students' purposeful and meaningful talk in the classroom. Our framework for defining emerging sophistication has been the profiles developed by Griffin, Smith, and Burrill (1995) based on the earlier work of Griffin (1989). A holistic view of language processes has been reinforced, and a paradigm created that supports the importance of the interaction that takes place when talk is added to the reading program. Most importantly, this study has demonstrated the use of assessment practices that are not detrimental either to the students or the teacher.

# References

Bakhtin, M.M. (1981). *The dialogic imagination: Four essays* (C. Emerson, Trans.). In M. Holquist (Ed.). Austin, TX: University of Texas Press.

Barnes, D., Britton, J., & Torbe, M. (1986). *Language, the learner and the school* (3rd ed.). Harmondsworth, UK: Penguin.

Chambers, A. (1993). *Tell me.* Stroud, UK: Thimble Press.

Dickinson, J. (1993). Children's perspectives on talk: Building a learning community. In C. Gilles (Ed.), *Cycles of meaning: Exploring the potential of talk in learning communities.* Portsmouth, NH: Heinemann.

Glaser, R. (1981). The future of testing: A research agenda for cognitive psychology and psychometrics. *American Psychologist, 18,* 9–23.

Griffin, P.E. (1989). Monitoring children's growth towards literacy. *Bulletin of Victorian Institute for Education Research (VIER), 61,* 45–72.

Griffin, P.E., Smith, P.G., & Burrill, L. (1995). *The American literacy profile scales.* Portsmouth, NH: Heinemann.

Griffin, P.E., & Nix, P. (1991). *Educational assessment and reporting.* Sydney, Australia: Harcourt Brace Jovanovich.

Langer, J.A. (1990). Understanding literature. *Language Arts, 67*(8), 812–816.

Mehan, H. (1979a). *Learning lessons.* Cambridge, MA: Harvard University Press.

Mehan, H. (1979b). What time is it Denise? Asking known information questions in classroom discourse. *Theory Into Practice, 28,* 285–294.

Messick, S. (1984). The interplay of evidence and consequences in the validation of performance assessments. *Educational Researcher, 23*(2), 13–23.

O'Flahavan, J.F., Hartman, D.H., & Pearson, P.D. (1988). Teacher questioning and feedback practices: A 20 year retrospective. In J. Readence & R. Baldwin (Eds.), *Dialogues in literacy research: The 37th yearbook of the National Reading Conference.* Chicago: National Reading Conference.

Peterson, R. (1992). *Life in a crowded place: Making a learning community.* Portsmouth, NH: Heinemann.

Rasch, G. (1960). *Some probabilistic models for the measurement of attainment and intelligence.* Chicago: MESA Press.

Vygotsky, L.S. (1971). *The psychology of art.* Cambridge, MA: MIT Press.

Vygotsky, L.S. (1978). *Mind in society: The development of higher psychological processes* (M. Cole, V.J. Steiner, S. Scribner, & E. Souberman, Eds. & Trans.). Boston: Harvard University Press. (Original work published 1934)

Wertsch, J.V. (1991). *Voices of the mind: A sociocultural approach to mediated action.* Hemel Hempstead, UK: Harvester Wheatsheaf.

## Children's Books Cited

Crew, G. (1992). *Lucy's bay* (Ill. G. Rogers). Queensland, Australia: Jam Roll Press.

Macdonald, C. (1993). *The lake at the end of the world.* Victoria, Australia: Puffin.

Marsden, J. *Out of time.* Victoria, Australia: Pan.

Sendak, M. (1988). Where the wild things are. New York: HarperCollins.

Van Allsburg, C. (1981). *Jumanji.* Boston: Houghton Mifflin.

Van Allsburg, C. (1985). *The Polar Express.* London: Andersen Press.

Van Allsburg, C. (1994). *The mysteries of Harris Burdick.* London: Andersen Press.

Wagner, J., & Brooks, R. (1977). *John Brown, Rose and the midnight cat.* London: Viking Kestrel.

# A Developmental Assessment Approach to Assessing and Reporting Students' Speaking Skills

*Margaret Forster*

It is Wednesday afternoon. The Grade 3 students are sitting on the mat at the front of the classroom. One wall of the room is covered with revised traditional tales based on Roald Dahl's *Revolting Rhymes*. Story artwork hangs from the ceiling. For 3 weeks the teacher has been reading folktales and fables from around the world and the students have been comparing the underlying messages of these texts. Yesterday afternoon they listened to a tape of an Aboriginal elder telling a local dreamtime legend and answered some questions about what they had heard. Last Wednesday they watched a video of an African story, *Why Mosquitoes Buzz in People's Ears*, and Jennifer's father visited to talk about growing up in Africa and the stories he heard as a child. All these activities are part of a carefully structured language arts program that is focused around a myths and legends theme.

The children look expectant. The teacher says, "Today we're going to do something a little different. Today we're going to tell stories. Today each of you is going to tell us one of your favorite stories. You will be working with a partner to practice your story and then you will be telling it to the rest of the class. I will be listening to how well you tell the story, what you say, and how interesting you make it for the audience. First of all, let's make a list of some of the stories you might like to choose."

The students brainstorm possibilities and the teacher lists their ideas on the chalkboard. During the discussion the teacher points out some of the difficulties involved in retelling a story—for example, it's difficult to keep an audience's interest with a long story; television programs are usually not suitable for successful storytelling. The teacher encourages students to pick well-known, self-contained stories such as *The Three Little Pigs* and *The Lion and the Mouse*. When there is an extensive list of possibilities on the chalkboard the teacher says, "With your partner, you are going to choose a story and then practice how you are going to tell it. It would be a good idea to practice twice. Once to make sure you've got the story clear, and the second time to think about how you could make your story more interesting for the audience. Your partner's job is to listen to you practice and help you organize your presentation. Let's think about some of the things you could do to make your story more interesting to listen to."

There is a short discussion about characterization, voices, and actions. The teacher reinforces that the task is to tell a well-known story in an interesting way, but not to make up a new story.

When the students have found a partner to work with, the teacher moves around the room labeling one student in each pair Partner 1 and the other student Partner 2. The teacher says, "Partner 1's raise your hands. Now it is time for all of you Partner 1's to choose a story and practice it. Partner 2, your job is to help your partner by making sure nothing is missing from their story and by making suggestions about how to make the presentation interesting. After you have practiced we will listen to all the people who are Partner 1 present their stories. So, Partner 2, do not rehearse your story yet. You will rehearse your story after we have heard all the Partner 1 stories. Partner 1, you have 10 minutes to organize your presentation."

The teacher lets the students know when they have 5 minutes left. She arranges the room so that everyone can see and hear each speaker's presentation.

The Partner 1's now present their stories in turn. The teacher makes evaluation notes as each student speaks, and praises each as they finish. When all Partner 1's have presented, the teacher and the class applaud. The teacher calls for a short break and reminds the students that Partner 2's will rehearse and present their stories soon.

After the break, the process of rehearsal, presentation, and teacher evaluation is repeated for Partner 2's. To complete the session there is a brief class discussion focusing on what makes a good story presentation.

This vignette is an introduction to one authentic and standardized speaking assessment task designed by the Australian Council for Educational Research (ACER). Teachers introduce the task by following the standardized directions in the Developmental Assessment Resource for Teachers (DART) administration manual (Bodey, et al., 1997), which provides teachers with a model for incorporating assessment in classroom learning. The middle elementary (grades 3 and 4) DART kit from which this speaking task comes equips teachers with authentic assessment tasks for reading, viewing, speaking, listening, and writing. The tasks are open-ended and require students to use high level reasoning skills as well as more basic literacy understandings.

The tasks in the middle elementary kit are contextualized in a myths and legends theme. A teacher using this kit can choose to administer the tasks as isolated assessments or to embed the tasks in the everyday curriculum. A teacher who follows the latter more "authentic" path focuses the language arts program for 4 to 6 weeks on the myths and legends theme and administers the standardized tasks at appropriate times during that period—bringing assessment and curriculum seamlessly together. The kit provides tasks, detailed scoring guides and rating scales, examples of students' work, diagnostic information about students' strengths and weaknesses, and report forms that illustrate students' levels of achievement numerically and descriptively.

DART is just one example of ACER's program of research to support teachers in their understanding of students' speaking growth. In developing these tasks ACER has provided teachers not only with practical assistance but also with a conceptual framework for assessing speaking in the classroom. ACER has also offered professional development in speaking assessment through the National School English Literacy Survey (NSELS), and offers tools in the form of published "progress maps" to help teachers understand the nature of speaking growth.

The ACER research takes a developmental assessment approach (Masters & Forster, 1996) to assessing and reporting students' speaking achievement. The principles underlying this approach form the structure of this chapter. Examples of the principles in action are taken from two sources: the DART materials and the 1996 NSELS. *Mapping Literacy Achievement* (Masters & Forster, 1997) details the principles, findings, and procedures of the 1996 NSELS. The report provides, for the first time in Australia, reliable baseline data mapping the broad range of literacy achievements among Grade 3 and Grade 5 students (typically aged 8 and 10 years) in Australian schools.

The survey was based on a broad definition of literacy with students' knowledge, skills, and understandings in reading, writing, viewing, listening, and speaking assessed. This approach served two purposes: to provide national data on a range of literacy achievements, and to emphasize to teachers the importance of assessing a broad range of literacy skills.

# Developmental Assessment

Developmental assessment is the process by which a student's level of achievement in an area of learning is assessed in order to decide the best ways to facilitate further learning. A developmental assessment approach is based on five principles that are as important to teacher–designed classroom assessments as they are to professionally developed standardized tasks:

Monitor students' growth against the learning outcomes of a progress map.

Consider a range of assessment methods to select an appropriate assessment method for the outcomes addressed.

Judge and record students' performances on assessment tasks.

Estimate students' levels of achievement against the levels of a progress map.

Report student achievement in terms of a progress map.

(Masters & Forster, 1996).

## *Monitor Students' Growth Against the Learning Outcomes of a Progress Map*

The first principle in developmental assessment is to monitor students' growth against a progress map. This map (also called a continuum, strand, or variable) describes growth in an area of learning—the knowledge, skills, understandings, attitudes, or values that students develop in an area of learning in the order in which they typically develop them. The indicators of growth along a progress map sometimes are called learning "outcomes" or "indicators."

An example of a progress map is shown in Figure 1. This map describes growth in the area of speaking and listening. The arrow indicates the direction of growth.

As well as providing a conceptual framework for understanding students' growth across the grades of school, a progress map provides a reference point for monitoring growth. This reference point is especially useful because it is independent of the particular instrument used to assess learning—in much the same way as a scale for height provides a reference point regardless of the instrument used to measure height.

The work at ACER to assess and monitor students' speaking growth is based on the progress map frameworks of the Australian national profiles. During the period 1990–1993, as part of a collaborative effort of all Australian states and territories and the Australian government, "statements" and "profiles" for eight areas of the school curriculum were developed ("English: A Curriculum Profile…" 1994). Each statement defines a learning area and describes a sequence for developing knowledge, skills, and understandings. Each accompanying profile provides a framework for reporting student achievement. Some states and territories revised these documents to produce their own versions, and others distributed and used them in their original form. In the United States, frameworks of this kind sometimes are called curriculum standards.

---

**FIGURE 1**
**A progress map in speaking and listening**

Analyze critically the relationship between texts, contexts, speakers, and listeners in a range of situations.

Compare and contrast the use of language in spoken texts that present different perspectives on complex themes and issues.

Discuss critically the spoken language use of others and select, prepare, and present spoken texts for specified purposes and audiences.

Listen critically, commenting on context, and adjust own speaking for different purposes, situations, and audience expectations.

Vary speaking and listening for a small range of contexts purposes and audiences.

Vary speaking and listening for familiar situations.

Use speaking and listening appropriately for classroom situations.

*Curriculum and Standards Framework II* (2nd ed.). (2000). Carlton, Victoria, Australia: The Board of Studies.

The Australian English profile is organized into three strands: Speaking and Listening, Reading and Viewing, and Writing. These strands correspond with the language modes of English. Each strand consists of a series of learning outcomes. Outcomes are descriptions of knowledge, skills, and understandings that students typically would develop in English. The outcomes are structured into four organizers or substrands: texts, contextual understandings, linguistic structures and features, and strategies. The organizers provide different ways of looking at students' performances:

*Texts* focuses on what students are doing with what kinds of texts.

*Contextual understanding* focuses on students' understanding of sociocultural and situational contexts.

*Linguistic structures and features* focuses on students' use of linguistic structures and features of text.

*Strategies* focuses on how students go about composing and comprehending text.

Within each profile strand (and substrand), outcomes are organized into eight levels. These levels are broadly defined ranges of achievement for the compulsory grades of school—8 levels for 10 grades of schooling.

In helping teachers to think about the relationship between the skills of speaking and listening as described in the profile, ACER suggests that teachers imagine speaking and listening along a continuum. At one end of the continuum is listening—for example, listening to the radio or a formal speech. At the other end of the continuum is speaking—for example, giving a speech or making announcements. In the middle of the continuum is interactive speaking and listening—for example, small-group discussion. Assessment tasks can be developed for each of these very different contexts.

ACER has developed standardized tasks and marking guides for the assessment of speaking, listening, and interactive speaking and listening in authentic classroom settings. These are available to teachers as part of the DART.

The assessments developed for the NSELS provide an example of materials that address profile outcomes. In the assessment of speaking, the following literacy outcomes, as defined by the Speaking and Listening strand of the profile, were addressed:

- uses spoken language effectively as required by the formal school environment,
- describes and explains ideas to others,
- expresses the main ideas in a text to others, and
- engages the listener.

In particular, outcomes from Levels 1, 2, 3, 4, and 5 of the Speaking and Listening strand were addressed including:

- interacts confidently with others in a variety of situations to develop and present familiar ideas, events, and information (Texts, Level 4);
- considers how own speaking and listening are adjusted to different situations (Contextual understanding, Level 2);
- usually uses linguistic structures and features of spoken language appropriately for expressing and interpreting ideas and information (Linguistic structures and features, Level 3); and
- assists and monitors the communication patterns of self and others (Strategies, Level 4).

(Masters & Forster, 1997, pp. 258–259)

When teachers are developing their own speaking tasks for classroom use they also need to address directly the outcomes of the progress map to which they are teaching. Which speaking skills are described in your curriculum and performance standards frameworks? Which learning outcomes would you address if you were developing speaking tasks?

### Consider a Range of Assessment Methods to Select an Appropriate Assessment Method for the Outcomes Addressed

The second principle in developmental assessment is to consider a range of assessment methods in order to select an appropriate method for the outcomes addressed. In developmental assessment, a teacher's records of student observations provide the evidence needed to estimate a student's level of achievement. These observations must be relevant. That is, they must provide evidence about the learning outcomes identified on a progress map. If they do not, then conclusions based on these observations will lack validity. In general, the larger the number of relevant observations the richer the evidence and the more dependable the conclusion about a student's current level of attainment.

When planning the collection of evidence, teachers need to select carefully the assessment method on which evidence of a student's achievement will be based. Different assessment methods will provide information about different types of outcomes. For example, if the outcomes addressed require evidence of students' abilities to write for a range of purposes and audiences, then a portfolio is the most appropriate assessment method. If the outcomes require evidence of students' abilities to collect, analyze, and report information then a project is the most appropriate assessment method.

ACER has developed support materials for teachers that explore the principles of developmental assessment and provide information about the range of assessment methods available. These materials, packaged as the ACER Assessment Resource Kit (ARK), come in easily accessible magazine and video format. The ARK currently includes seven titles: Developmental Assessment, Progress Maps, Portfolios, Performances, Products, Projects, and Paper and Pen, as well as a video introducing the principles of developmental assessment and a workshop manual. Further titles are under development.

In the NSELS survey, outcomes were addressed using a range of methods including paper-and-pen assessment, portfolio assessment, and in the case of speaking, performance assessment—on-the-spot observations of students as they were speaking. Evidence of students' speaking achievements was collected from two sources: observations of speaking performances on standardized speaking tasks ("common tasks"), and records of observations of students' classroom speaking ("best work"). (Masters & Forster, 1997, pp. 258–259)

To maximize the authenticity of the tasks and to model thematic approaches to learning, the survey common tasks were presented in integrated settings, with the intention that they could be embedded in teachers' curricula and accompanied by thematic scaffolding activities for students. Literacy tasks for Grade 3 students were based on a "myths and legends" theme with all tasks loosely integrated around a central videotape and picture book. Literacy tasks for Grade 5 students were built around a film titled "Looking for Space Things" (Armstrong, no date). The tasks were administered using standardized instructions within a 4- to 6-week period.

For the speaking assessment, students completed two common tasks: narrative presentation (telling a story or a poem to entertain) and argument/opinion presentation (offering an opinion to convince a listener). Grade 3 students retold their favorite narrative and reviewed a character from the provided videotape. Grade 5 students talked about their favorite television show and discussed a poem in small groups in preparation for individual presentation and commentary. Each individual presentation was preceded by guided small-group discussion.

Individual presentations required students to consider the ways in which spoken text is used to communicate meaning through content of presentation (quality of ideas and ability to justify opinions) and performance elements (awareness of and ability to engage the audience).

Students' best work in speaking was assembled by teachers in three specified categories. Teachers based their assessments on two speaking performances/presentations: a reflective/discursive piece (personal narrative, or a response to an issue, e.g., morning talk or debate); and either an imaginative piece (e.g., narrative, poem, or play) or a piece from a subject area other than English (e.g., a science report, an individual project, or a report on a group activity in mathematics). Teachers provided records made at the time of these presentations or video or audio recordings of the presentations if they were available.

When teachers are planning to collect evidence of students' speaking achievement in their own classrooms, they need to consider the most appropriate method. What assessment method(s) would you use when addressing speaking outcomes described in your curriculum and performance standards?

## Judge and Record Students' Performances on Assessment Tasks

The third principle in developmental assessment is to judge and record students' performances on assessment tasks. Teachers use a variety of methods to judge and record students' work. Some records indicate whether tasks have been completed correctly, others record partial understandings. Sometimes ratings of student work are recorded, either based on separate judgments of aspects of a piece of work (analytic ratings) or based on single overall (holistic) ratings.

ACER has presented an analytic rating scale model to assist teachers in assessing students' speaking skills. Two aspects of speaking are assessed separately: the quality of the content (understanding of ideas and ability to justify opinions) and the quality of the performance (awareness of audience and ability to engage audience). It is important for teachers to separate these qualities of student work in the same way as they would separate the quality of ideas in a piece of writing from surface features of language such as spelling, punctuation, and grammar. For example, a student might have excellent ideas organized in a well-structured report but speak in a soft, deadpan way that does not engage the audience. Another student might be hugely entertaining but have very little to say about a topic. Following are examples of two different teachers' observations of two different students' speaking performances. Notice how the first attends primarily to performance elements, the second to both content and performance elements.

First Teacher:
    Topic: Softball
    Time: 45 seconds
    animated presentation
    read, rather than refer to notes at times
    showed softball uniform and equipment
    audience eye contact most of the time
    clear speech, good expression and volume

Second Teacher:
    Joannah is a member of the school debating team
    very detailed
    covers many aspects of topic
    main issues introduced and explored in detail
    uses personal experiences to add to the presentation

issues supported by evidence

rebuttal was well presented and thought out

use of palm cards for prompt only

regularly looking at and engaging audience

loud clear voice

well-modulated

pauses added for effect

(Masters & Forster, 1997, pp. 153–155)

In the assessment of the NSELS common task speaking, teachers were given a set of described rating levels. The levels were constructed to correspond with Levels 1 to 5 of the English profile. That is, rating descriptions at each level were constructed to address outcomes of the profile at each level.

Grade 3 teachers were given Levels 1 to 4 only in their assessment guides; Grade 5 teachers, Levels 2 to 5. The rating levels were used to make on-the-spot judgments of common task performances. Separate rating levels were provided for content and performance. The guide to Level 4 (Content and Performance) for one of the Grade 3 speaking tasks is shown here. Teachers did not create a checklist of the features of a student's performance but made a best-fit judgment of a level of achievement.

Excerpt From Speaking (Common Task) Assessment Guide

Level 4 Content
Presents a strong point of view about the characters or their favorite character. Justifies opinion beyond narrative interpretation. (e.g., "I like python because of his power.")

Level 4 Performance
Speaks clearly and articulately (allowing for some hesitation) with good natural expression

AND

has a good, consistent sense of audience.

(Bodey, et al., 1997, p. 272)

Teachers were given similar rating levels for use in judging "best work" records of speaking performances. For each best-work category, teachers were given a category-specific guide to the assessment of Content. The Performance rating levels were the same as for the common tasks. To ensure the teachers developed a shared understanding of the rating levels, assessment guides were accompanied by annotated samples of student work. The guide to Level 4 for the Reflective/Discursive category is shown here.

Excerpt From Speaking (Best Work) Assessment Guide

Level 4 Reflective/Discursive category

Level statement:

Consistent attempts are made to justify opinions/assertions and include reasoned arguments.

Students may begin to experiment with relevant language and/or organizational elements of genre/topic.

Presentation is well organized.

Content:

Presents a strong point of view.

Offers some considered reasons or arguments.

Performance:

Speaks clearly and articulately (allowing for some hesitation) with good natural expression

AND

has a good, consistent sense of audience.

(Bodey, et al, 1997, p. 272)

Because it was particularly important that teachers' judgments were comparable, teachers in the survey were trained carefully. A series of workshops provided the 900 participating teachers with handbooks for "hands-on" practice in assessing reading, writing, and listening; viewing work samples; and using assessment guides and record sheets. For speaking assessment, teachers viewed a series of videotaped speaking performances and completed guided and unassisted practice sessions. To maximize comparability across teachers and schools, speaking assessments were made collaboratively by teachers and expert assessors.

When teachers plan to judge and record evidence of students' speaking achievement in their own classrooms, they need to consider carefully the aspects of the speaking skill about which they will make judgments, and consider the best method for judging and recording student work. What aspects of students' speaking skills do you consider when you are assessing speaking achievement?

## Estimate Students' Levels of Achievement Against the Levels of a Progress Map

The fourth principle in developmental assessment is to estimate students' achievement against the levels of a progress map. Because a progress map is a description of the path students typically follow as they progress through an area of learning, the records made for any particular student may only resemble this path. An on-balance assessment of the student's level of achievement will need to be made. The quality of this estimate will depend on the validity of the observations on which the estimate is based, on the reliability of the estimate (the amount of evidence), and on the objectivity of the estimate—whether the estimate is unaffected by the choice of task and assessor.

In NSELS, because the levels of the speaking rating scales were constructed to correspond to levels of the progress map, each rating provided a direct estimate of the student's location on the map. For example, a student whose speaking performance was rated at Level 4 was estimated to be performing at Level 4 of the English Profile in speaking. To increase the reliability of the estimates, students' performances on two tasks were considered.

Professionally developed assessment tasks that address learning outcomes in a progress map can provide teachers with a model for making on-balance estimates of student achievement. They also can provide teachers with additional evidence of student achievement to complement other less formal evidence they collect in the classroom. On what basis do you estimate students' levels of speaking achievement? Do you use any professionally designed assessment tasks?

## Report Student Achievement in Terms of a Progress Map

The fifth and last principle in developmental assessment is to report student achievement in terms of a progress map. In developmental assessment, because students' growth is assessed and monitored against a described continuum, students' estimated locations on a progress map can be reported descriptively in terms of the knowledge, skills, understandings, attitudes, or values typically demonstrated by students at these locations.

In NSELS, Grade 3 and Grade 5 students' achievements were reported descriptively and graphically against a series of survey scales. The achievements of students from a number of subgroups were reported also: males and females; students from English and non-English speaking backgrounds; students from low, medium, and high socioeconomic backgrounds; and students from the special indigenous sample. In the case of speaking, achievements on common tasks and best work were reported separately and in combination.

The NSELS speaking scale is illustrated in Figure 2. The scale, which describes increasing achievement in speaking, is empirically based. That is, it is based on an analysis of observed student performances. The cluster of indicators at Level 1 of the profile describes the lowest level of achievement in speaking in the survey. The cluster of indicators at Level 5 of the profile describes the highest level of achievement in speaking in the survey. The italicized indicators describe performance elements (awareness of an audience and ability to engage the audience).

Descriptions of the knowledge, skills, and understandings typically demonstrated by students at various levels along the scale are provided. Below these descriptions are transcripts of students' performances on the common tasks, one

---

## FIGURE 2
### Illustrating the Survey Speaking Scale

---

**Speaking Level 1**

Students working at this level typically are able to express ideas simply and to convey limited meaning (e.g., using "and" and "then" and repeating words); and present a talk that contains some unrelated ideas (may need prompting); is disjointed or incomplete (may need prompting); demonstrates a limited understanding of the speaking task (may stray from original intent); *demonstrates a limited understanding of the need to communicate with the audience; and is inaudible at times.*

My picture's…like…um…he puts sticks in his ears.

Two percent of Grade 3 students are working at or below this level.

**Speaking Level 2**

Students working at this level typically are able to tell a story with a recognizable plot; offer one or two comments or opinions, but with little or no justification; include some key information; demonstrate a basic understanding of a speaking task; and give a presentation that *is audible but shows little sense of addressing audience (e.g., may be little eye contact where culturally appropriate);* is largely incomplete or long and unstructured (some content may be irrelevant); *and displays little attempt to modulate voice.*

Um… my favorite character is rabbit because he is a fast runner and he is a goodie (giggles).

Twenty six percent of Grade 3 students and 7% of Grade 5 students are working at or below this level.

**Speaking Level 3**

Students working at this level typically are able to tell a complete story with a logical plot but lacking in detail; give a full account of a character, experience, or event including all key information; show some evidence of organization (presentation may be muddled or incomplete); justify an opinion with mostly descriptive information; offer a few arguments, mostly assertions; and *speak clearly and articulately (allowing for some hesitation) with good natural expression but with little awareness of audience.*

My favorite character is the owl because the owl woke up the sun every day. And my picture shows when the rabbit and the monkey and everything and the stick landed on the bird, and him dying, and the snake and the rabbit getting out of his hole. And I thought the baddie…um…the baddie was the mosquito because he bothered everyone and no one liked him and the iguana put sticks in his ears to ignore him.

Fifty-five percent of Grade 3 students and 50% of Grade 5 students are working at this level.

**Speaking Level 4**

Students working at this level typically are able to present a complete and well-organized account (e.g., a well-rounded story including details); attempt to justify assertions (e.g., "It's a funny show because of the way…"); attempt to generalize about aspects of a topic (e.g., include a synopsis of a show, as opposed to telling one episode); present a strong point of view (e.g., about a favorite character); *speak clearly and articulately (allowing for some hesitation) with good natural expression; and display a good, consistent sense of audience.*

Good afternoon. Um…my picture…um…is showing where the lizard's drinking water and the mosquito's coming to bother it and to tell it lies, and the iguana puts sticks in its ears. And I think that the…um…mosquito shouldn't have told lies but it wasn't necessarily at fault for doing all the rest and everything. And…um…I think the lion was a wonderful, a good character because he helped solve the problem and helped everyone to figure out and he didn't blame anyone until he found out the person who actually did

*(continued)*

---

**FIGURE 2**
**Illustrating the Survey Speaking Scale (continued)**

---

it. And I liked, I liked the monkey as well as the iguana because I liked the way it broke the branch and it fell on the owl and that's all.

Seventeen percent of Grade 3 students are working at or above this level and 38% of Grade 5 students are working at this level.

**Speaking Level 5**

Students working at this level typically are able to present a well-reasoned account; display a sense of key issues; effectively use appropriate language and/or organizational elements appropriate to genre; consistently enhance presentation with relevant details; give considered reasons for opinions (generally justify assertions); and *begin to engage audience through language, gesture, and tone.*

The bit that I picked was the last one and I picked it because I thought it talked about the poorer people and I'm concerned about them 'cos they're less fortunate than us. Um, a bit that John Paul said he thought was funny was that he only took the loaf of bread. Because the man was really hungry so he didn't take anything valuable. He knew he couldn't sell it and so he just took the loaf of bread. The last bit says, "Sitting by the fire I made toast, two buttered pieces each, but I couldn't eat for thoughts of the hungry man keeping warm with sheep." As I said before, I chose it because it talks about the poorer people in our community that haven't got enough to eat. They keep warm—well this was the olden days—so he would keep warm—and this was the country—by being near the sheep.

Five percent of Grade 5 students are working at or above this level.

---

for each of the five levels of achievement described on the Speaking scale. The description and transcript together illustrate what students are typically able to do at each level of achievement. The percentages of Grade 3 and Grade 5 students working at each level are shown also.

The first four transcripts are examples of students' responses to a task in which they drew a scene incorporating their favorite character from a film they were shown and spoke about their choice to the class. The last transcript is a response to a task in which students read and discussed a poem and then spoke to the class about the section of the poem that most interested them.

The descriptions of student achievement at each level on the survey reporting scale can be used as a focus for teacher–student and teacher–parent discussions of progress, and to identify the kinds of learning activities likely to be most useful at particular stages in students' learning.

# Conclusion

Although ACER's work in the area of speaking assessment is Australian, it is relevant to all teachers who are interested in assessing and reporting students' speaking and other literacy skills. In general, this work has established that it is possible to provide models for the collection, in authentic contexts, of valid and reliable evidence about students' speaking skills. In particular, NSELS has demonstrated that it is possible to use national surveys as a context for professional development. NSELS also has demonstrated that if teachers are trained and supported to make comparable judgments of student achievement, and checking procedures are in place, then it is possible to collect reliable national data with teachers taking a central role.

Finally, what we have learned in Australia about the speaking achievements of Grade 3 and Grade 5 students also should be of interest. It is likely that the most significant finding of the survey would be replicated in surveys elsewhere: At each Grade level, there is a considerable difference between the achievements of the lowest and highest achieving students. The top 10% of students at each Grade are about five Grade levels ahead of the bottom 10%.

At the highest level of speaking achievement, 5% of Grade 5 students are able to present challenging ideas; give considered reasons for their opinions; and begin to engage the audience through language, gesture, and tone. A further 38% of Grade 5 students and 17% of Grade 3 students make spoken presentations that are complete and well organized. They speak clearly and articulately, present a strong point of view, and display a good consistent sense of audience.

At the lowest level of speaking achievement, 2% of Grade 3 students are able to do little more than present a few ideas simply, perhaps inaudibly, in a disjointed and incomplete manner. A further 26% of Grade 3 students, and 7% of Grade 5 students include some key information in their presentation, demonstrate a basic understanding of the speaking task, and are audible, but show little sense of addressing the audience.

With conceptual frameworks for assessing and reporting speaking achievement in place, with tools to support teacher assessment of speaking provided, and with the range of students' speaking achievements mapped, the challenge for teachers, schools, and administrators is to work to raise all students' levels of achievement.

To return to a classroom setting where we began, but this time to a Grade 5 class where a student has just completed a standardized speaking task, here is one Grade 5 student's response.

> My favorite TV show is the um (looks very nervous, shuffles feet)….The name of the class…um show is *The Simpsons*. It is funny. (Looks at notes, bites lip.) It is funny. (Shuffles feet and looks at the ceiling.) It is funny and easy to understand. It is on (looks at notes) 6:00 every week night. (Looks at notes and reads), I like the show because (lowers notes)….My family thinks it's OK for us kids and her name is Lisa Simpson (looks at the ceiling). I like her because she plays the saxophone. She's funny and (checks notes again, smiles)….She's special to me because I think she's funny.

At what level on your standards framework is this student's speaking skill? How would you help this student to progress? What learning activities do you think would be appropriate for a student at this level of speaking achievement?

## References

Armstrong, J., (Writer & Director). (no date). *Looking for space things* [Film]. Australian Film Institute Distribution, Ltd.

Bodey, W., Darkin, L., Forster, M., & Masters, G. (1997). *DART English Middle Primary.* Camberwell, Australia: The Australian Council for Educational Research.

*Curriculum and Standards Framework II* (2nd ed.). (2000). Carlton, Victoria, Australia: The Board of Studies.

Department of Employment, Education and Training. (1991). *Australia's language: The Australian Language and Literacy Policy.* Canberra, Australia: Australian Government Publishing Service.

*English: A curriculum profile for Australian schools.* (1994). Carlton, Australia: Curriculum Corporation.

Masters, G.N., & Forster, M. (1996). *ARK Developmental Assessment.* Melbourne, Australia: ACER.

Masters, G.N., & Forster, M. (1997). *Mapping literacy achievement: Results of the 1996 National School English Literacy Survey.* Commonwealth of Australia: Department of Employment, Education, Training and Youth Affairs.

*Note:* Page numbers followed by *f* indicate figures; those followed by *t* indicate tables.

## D

DEBATING, 66, 67*f*

DECONTEXTUALIZED LANGUAGE, 30—31

DEMONSTRATION: in language learning, 37—38, 39—40; in SAID framework, 39—40

DEVELOPMENTAL ASSESSMENT, 143—153; judging and recording performance in, 148—150; learning outcomes in, 144; learning profiles in, 144—145; methodology for, 146—148; progress maps in, 143—144, 144*f*, 150—153; survey scales in, 151—153, 152*f*—153*f*

DEVELOPMENTAL ASSESSMENT RESOURCE FOR TEACHERS (DART), 142, 145

DEVELOPMENTAL PSYCHOLOGY PERSPECTIVE: on oral language, 15*t*, 17—18

DIALECT, 10

DIALOGUE: classroom, 7—9. *See also* School talk; language as, 3, 6—7

DISCOURSE: extended, 30—31; institutional, 21—22; narrative, 3—5, 63—66, 64*f*, 65*f*, 82

DISCOURSE THEORY, 21

DISCOVERY-BASED LEARNING, 18

DISCUSSION GROUPS: assessment and, 129—135; in ESL instruction, 49—53, 53*f*

DISTAR, 16

DRAWING: in ESL instruction, 43—49, 45*f*, 47*f*, 48*f*

## E

EDUCATION. *See also* language education; banking model of, 7

EMOTIONAL EXPRESSION: role plays and, 62—63

ENGLISH AS A SECOND LANGUAGE. *See* ESL instruction

EPISTEMOLOGICAL SILENCE, 83

ESL INSTRUCTION, 42—55; art in, 43—44, 43—49, 45*f*, 47*f*, 48*f*; family tree in, 44—46, 45*f*; learning environments in, 44—46; literature study groups in, 49—53, 53*f*; memory bubble in, 46, 47*f*; personal scrapbook in, 46—49; storyboard drawings in, 46, 48*f*

EXPERIENTIAL STRUCTURE, 6

EXTEMPORANEOUS SPEAKING, 66

EXTENDED DISCOURSE, 30—31

## F

FAMILY TREE: in ESL instruction, 44—46, 45*f*

FIELDS, 22

FIGURATIVE LANGUAGE, 80

## G–H

GROUPING METHODS, 59

HABITUS, 22

HETEROGENEOUS GROUPING, 59

HOME TALK, 29—31; vs. school talk, 31—32, 105—107

HOMOGENEOUS GROUPING, 59

## I

IMAGING, 133—135

INITIATE-RESPOND-FEEDBACK PATTERN: alternatives to, 128—129, 129—135; in reading conference, 117